Looking for Steinbeck's Ghost

John Steinbeck with Charley behind the summer home on Bluff Point, near Sag Harbor, Long Island, New York, 1962. UPI Photo. Courtesy of the James S. Copley Library, La Jolla, California.

Looking for
Steinbeck's Ghost

By

Jackson J. Benson

UNIVERSITY OF OKLAHOMA PRESS : NORMAN AND LONDON

By Jackson J. Benson

Hemingway: The Writer's Art of Self-Defense (Minneapolis, 1969)

(Editor) *Hemingway in Our Time* (with Richard Astro) (Corvallis, Oreg., 1974)

(Editor) *The Short Stories of Ernest Hemingway: Critical Essays* (Durham, N.C., 1975)

(Editor) *The Fiction of Bernard Malamud* (with Richard Astro) (Corvallis, Oreg., 1977)

The True Adventures of John Steinbeck, Writer (New York, 1984)

Looking for Steinbeck's Ghost (Norman, 1988)

For good friends:
Dick and Jan Allman and
Dick and Starr Davis

Library of Congress Cataloging-in-Publication Data

Benson, Jackson J.
  Looking for Steinbeck's ghost.

  Includes index.
    1. Steinbeck, John, 1902–1968—Biography.
2. Novelists, American—20th century—Biography.
3. Biography—Technique. 4. Benson, Jackson J.
I. Title.
PS3537.T3234Z615 1988   813′.52 [B]   88-40205
ISBN 0-8061-2155-6 (alk. paper)

The paper in this book meets the guidelines for permanence and durability of the Committee on Production Guidelines for Book Longevity of the Council on Library Resources, Inc.

Contents

Illustrations

Preface

This collection of character sketches, nonfiction stories, and essays roughly follows the chronology of a fifteen-year effort to write the authorized biography of one of America's best-known and most-beloved authors. As one who never wrote a biography before and who did not set out to write one, I was totally unprepared for the snares and pitfalls that lay before me. This is partly the story of my misadventures and my education.

But it is also once again John Steinbeck's story—this time in brief and told largely by rebound and reflection, as we meet a girl friend of his college days, each of his three wives, his mother-in-law, and the man most responsible for the content of *The Grapes of Wrath*.

Most of all, however, this book is the story of a search through appearances to find an essence. It is an attempt to sift through all the testimony, all the contradictions, all the prejudice, favorable and unfavorable, to find out just who, at bottom, John Steinbeck was and what it was, if anything, he left to us as his legacy.

La Mesa, California   JACKSON J. BENSON

Acknowledgments

Part of "The Biographer as Detective," was first published in the April, 1976, issue of the *Journal of Modern Literature* as "The Background of *The Grapes of Wrath*," © 1976, Temple University. The "Kate" part of "Gwyn and Kate: Two Women in His Life" was first published in the *Stanford Magazine*, Spring, 1985, as "John and Kate: A Tale of Two Artists," © 1985, The Stanford Alumni Association. Part of "Pride and Prejudice" was first published as "Through a Political Glass, Darkly: The Example of John Steinbeck" in the Spring, 1984, issue of *Studies in American Fiction*, © 1984, Northeastern University. "Epilogue: The Spirit of a Writer" first appeared as "Hemingway the Hunter and Steinbeck the Farmer" in the Summer, 1985, issue of the *Michigan Quarterly Review*, © 1985, The University of Michigan. My thanks to these publications for permissions to reprint.

Permission to quote from John Steinbeck's works and letters in the above essays and stories has been given by McIntosh and Otis, Inc., agents acting for the John Stein-·beck estate.

Permission to quote from the letters and manuscripts of Katherine Beswick has been given by Department of Special Collections and University Archives, Stanford University Libraries.

J. J. B.

Looking for Steinbeck's Ghost

Ah, but to play man number one,
To drive the dagger in his heart,

To lay his brain upon the board
And pick the acrid colors out,

To nail his thought across the door,
Its wings spread wide to rain and snow,

To strike his living hi and ho,
To tick it, tock it, turn it true. . . .

      —Wallace Stevens,
      "The Man with the Blue Guitar"

Prologue: Would You Trust This Man?

Eight months before John Steinbeck died in December, 1968, I started on a journey, only I didn't know it at the time. It would be a journey that would take me away from my family every evening and every weekend for months, and then years, that would impose a burden that much of the time seemed almost impossible to bear, and that held out a goal, a destination, that as I approached seemed always to recede into the distance. I would seek and learn a great deal about John Steinbeck, but I would also learn about the world and about myself.

That I didn't even know at the beginning that I had started on my journey is typical of my naïveté. I think I have always been behind in life, not catching on to what's happening until it is all over, not achieving the age of eighteen until I was thirty and finding it was too late to have the adventures I should have had at eighteen. If a strong opinion should be voiced, I have always been able to voice it three or four hours after the event, in my mind. I probably have lived too much in my mind, in my reading and daydreams. So what I had embarked on, unknowingly at first, was a slow awakening to life itself, a birth, with all the trauma of being pushed out of a protective womb.

I suppose my naïveté has come, at least in part, out of my being an academic, but that, ironically, became also the agency for change. I am a teacher of American literature at a college, and it is part of my job to write books about American authors. My journey really began when I started out to write a critical assessment of John Steinbeck's work. I

3

picked Steinbeck because I had developed a special regard for his fiction over the years and because I thought that it had become greatly undervalued.

One reason for my special regard was that I was a third-generation Californian. Steinbeck has written about my country and my people. Although I grew up in San Francisco, I can remember traveling with my mother from one rural small town to another around the state. She was the home economics editor for a farm paper, the *Pacific Rural Press*, and part of her job was to go to farming communities and give cooking demonstrations, usually in the school auditorium or the American Legion hall, which featured products advertised in the paper. Although I was very young at the time, I can look back in my memory and see her, a very small woman determinedly practicing the principles of good public speaking, learned in school or from a book, on a large audience of skeptical farm women. They must have doubted that a young woman from the city, not too many years out of college, could tell *them* anything about cooking. But she had had practice with skeptical audiences. Her first job was teaching cooking and home management to the Klamath Indians while she was working for the Interior Department.

Those trips came during the thirties, but I don't remember seeing or even hearing about Okies. My mother, however, remembers how upset her editor would get at the very mention of the name Steinbeck. I suppose his attitude rubbed off on her, for although she was (and still is) the soul of tolerance, I remember feeling a vague tinge of unexpressed disapproval that hung in the air when, several years later, I accidentally discovered Steinbeck's books. I might have imagined this, since I also remember that she was usually delighted to have me reading anything at all. On the other hand, my uncle became so excited by his reading of *The Grapes of Wrath* that he went off looking for the Joads. At the time the book came out, he was a law student at the University of Oklahoma, and he spent his vacation hitchhiking round the state trying to find them. He did, too, not in Oklahoma, but in Arkansas just on the other side of the state line from Sallisaw.

From the few times I went with my mother on her rounds, I got an early sense of the land and the people outside the city. I could never quite imagine what the heaths and moors of England that I read so much about looked like, but I knew the rocky cliffs of the California shoreline; the round, brown hills of its coastal ranges; and the dairy and grass smells of the San Joaquin Valley. These impressions were embellished and reinforced by trips to the northern California woods, where my father, for several years at the beginning of my life, was the constable of a small lumber town (my parents were separated by the economics of the time but lucky in that they both had jobs), and later by trips at least once a year through the Central Valley to vacations in the southern Sierra Nevada.

I could at age eight or nine, and still can, recite the names of the valley towns that we drove by or through—Tracy, Manteca, Modesto, Turlock, Merced, Madera, Fresno, Visalia. They are burned on my brain from hours of impatient waiting in the back seat of our old Plymouth for each town to appear. The distance from Modesto to Fresno was almost unbearable, as the hot valley air streamed in the car windows and made the horsehair seats give off a dusty, dead smell that I still associate with car sickness. Outside each town, promising relief from the heat and tedium, was a fruit-juice stand, Giant Orange, which was shaped like an orange and painted so brightly that your mouth watered spontaneously. Each Giant Orange was visible for miles along the flat valley floor, but my entreaties were always ignored as my father drove straight on. During the Depression one did not spend money on frivolous things like orange juice at a stand when oranges could be purchased and squeezed for less than half the cost. My father ignored my argument that we had neither oranges nor squeezer now, when we really needed them.

I would settle back to watch the heat mirages take shape on the black asphalt—ponds, rivers, even trees took shape in the haze and then disappeared. The ascent from the valley to the high mountains and the smells of pine and skunk cabbage, the sudden rush of cool air, was almost literally a climb out of hell to heaven. We went to the Sierra so my dad could fly-fish, a skill he learned as a teenager working as a guide for English sportsmen in the wilds of northern California and southern Oregon.

I also had developed a special regard for Steinbeck because my first taste of serious modern American fiction came with the reading of his work. As a young teenager I picked one of his novels off the shelf of the public library, at random, without knowing who the author was. I had heard the name, but it meant little to me. I went on to read *The Long Valley, Tortilla Flat, Of Mice and Men, The Grapes of Wrath,* and later *Cannery Row.* These works made a great impression on me, first, because they were my own discovery. I never read them in school, nor had anyone recommended them to me. Second, they were very different from the nineteenth-century English and American novels we had on our bookshelves at home and were being assigned in school (we did have one modern American novel in high school—Booth Tarkington's *The Magnificent Ambersons*). It was a shock moving from *Adam Bede* to *Of Mice and Men,* like moving from a book place to a place close to home. Reading Steinbeck's books changed my sense of literature.

Many years later as a college professor, I was determined to "save" my writer from the savage scorn of mocking critics. With this more romantic than academic impulse, I set off on my foolish quest. It never occurred to me that there was no reason why eminent literary critics should listen to me or that a publication by an unknown scholar in a provincial university would be likely to convince professors at Columbia, Harvard, and Berkeley that Steinbeck, whom they considered below notice, should be taken seriously. I had no idea of where I was going with the project but simply stumbled forward, and with vague good intentions I began to reread all of Steinbeck's writings and to collect and read everything I could get hold of that had been written about him.

I had no idea of writing a biography or of spending a major portion of my life doing so. No one in his right mind sets out to spend fifteen years researching and writing a book—it just sneaks up on you. Through a series of misunderstandings and my own confusion, I just drifted into the job of becoming an authorized biographer. Much of the blame can be put on my mother-in-law.

She knew that I was working on a book on Steinbeck, and one day, without preface, she asked me if I'd like to meet one of the author's sisters. She explained that a good friend of hers also knew the sister very well and would be glad to arrange a meeting for me. I was writing a book of literary criticism and not planning on conducting any interviews, but I thought to myself it certainly wouldn't do any harm to talk to her. So I took a weekend to drive the 450 miles up to Pacific Grove, near Monterey, to see her, praying as I drove that my broken-down, rusty bus would make the trip. I am very conscientious, and my greatest concern as I listened carefully to every vibration of the air-cooled engine behind me was that I not get stuck on the road somewhere and be unable to meet my Monday morning classes.

I am also very literary-minded, and my worries about breaking down on highway 99, driving up the Central Valley, reminded me inevitably of the Joads and their terrible journey across from Oklahoma, through the desert, and eventually up the valley on this same highway. I had never gone through anything like that ordeal, of course, but I had been relatively poor for a long time, through a long period of graduate school and then many years as a teacher on a very low salary, and it seemed that I had spent much of my life in old cars, with a knot in my stomach from worrying about whether or not I could make it to the next town. I had learned early a lesson that seemed to me to relate to what Steinbeck had been talking about in some of his early novels: if your car breaks down out on the open road miles from anywhere, there are only two kinds of people that will stop and help—the young and the poor. Usually help had come to me from families of Mexican-Americans. I have tried over the years to repay my debts by stopping for others in trouble, but now I drive a new car, and I'm too frightened to stop very often.

When I went to see Steinbeck's sister for the first time, I didn't know a great deal about the writer's life. He had written little that was autobiographical and had refused, on those few occasions that he had been interviewed, to talk about himself. What was in print, therefore, was very sketchy, but I did know that I was about to visit the famous "11th Street house," the house which had figured prominently in the impoverished years of the writer's early career, the house he had lived in during the time when he was closest to Ed Ricketts, the "Doc" of *Cannery Row.*

When I got to Pacific Grove, I had a hard time finding the house, and I was beginning to get nervous about the meeting. I drove up and down the street several times before discovering that the house doesn't face the street at all; the entrance faced what once had been a backyard. What one sees from the street are the nearly blank wooden walls of the back and side of the house and a high wooden fence painted to match. Much later I realized that the anonymity of the house in its presentation to the street reflected Steinbeck's continual search for privacy, for it was he, back in the 1930s, who had remodeled his parents' vacation home, walling in the sleeping porches and putting the entry in the back. I would find that almost all of the houses he owned over his lifetime had this same unprepossessing quality and were difficult to find unless you knew where to look.

By the time I met the sister, Mrs. E. G. Ainsworth, her brother had been dead almost two years, and I was two and a half years into my project of writing a Steinbeck critique. She was a hearty, energetic woman in her mid-seventies who took away my nervousness and made me feel welcome right away. As we stood for a moment at the door, she pointed to the garden that John had developed and the

The entry to the 11th Street house, Pacific Grove, California. Photograph by Richard L. Allman.

fishpond he had made. It was clear from the beautifully
trimmed and cared-for plantings, mostly fuchsias, and the
rich black soil that an affection for gardening ran in the family. As we entered, she also had me note the little Mexican-
style fireplace that her brother had built. We sat and talked
that first day for several hours, punctuated by a lunch of
homemade chicken-and-barley soup. I could see from her
attitude and what she was telling me about her brother that
she assumed that I was writing a biography of some sort.
When I left, she told me that, whatever I did, she hoped
that I would not write one of those huge books, one of those
terribly long biographies that were impossible to read. I as-
sured her I had nothing of the sort in mind.

I went to visit Mrs. Ainsworth on several more occasions,
and always she seemed to act on the basis that I would be
working on her brother's life story. I said nothing, for by
this time I wasn't sure what I was going to do. During one
visit she offered to show me around Salinas, and so on a
windy spring day, billowing white clouds scudding across
the sky, we drove the fifteen miles inland. We stopped first
at the cemetery, where she showed me the Hamilton plot
(John's mother's family) and where John's ashes were bur-
ied. On this day it appeared to be something of an informal
shrine, for there were several bouquets on the marker,
three or four vases and a water glass of drooping, home-
grown flowers, as well as several single flowers that had
been placed here and there. Mrs. Ainsworth herself had
come with flowers, for it had been John's birthday a few
weeks earlier, and she had been unable, until now, to get
over to visit the grave. She asked if I could leave her for a
half hour or so, which I did.

I wondered at the time whether the tributes on the
marker had come from friends and relatives or whether
they were the offerings of strangers, tourists passing
through. In looking back now, I'm inclined to think they
came from tourists rather than from Salinas folk. Some of
the old antagonism for their Nobel Prize–winning son still

lingers on, and there is a sort of perverse pride that the wound has not yet healed. Pauline Pearson, who has worked with the John Steinbeck Library, taping interviews with old-timers and locating historical sites, tells of the time when she took a group of Steinbeck enthusiasts on a tour of local points of interest. The bus stopped at the cemetery, and Pauline led several dozen people to the family plot and John's marker, where she began to give a little talk about the author's death and burial. She spoke about the service in New York, about Elaine, John's widow, bringing the ashes to Pacific Grove, and about a second service for family and friends on Point Lobos. After a few minutes, right in the middle of her presentation, the sprinklers suddenly came on all around the group, getting everyone wet and soaking to the skin several of the group that didn't move fast enough. Some groundskeeper was apparently registering his protest that John Steinbeck should be revered in this way by outsiders.

When I left Mrs. Ainsworth, I had nowhere to go, so I simply drove down the street, out of sight, and waited. On my return we continued our tour, and she had me drive around to the area of Salinas which had been the red-light district during the time of the action in *East of Eden*. There was little more to see than a row of small, one-story Victorian frame houses, most of which had at some time been painted white. Then we drove over to the Steinbeck family home, which was being used as a headquarters for the Hartnell College Newman Club (it had been left to the club in the previous owner's will). We couldn't go in but instead sat in the car while Mrs. Ainsworth pointed to various rooms and told me about her life there as a child, her parents, and her problems in taking care of her younger brother. He was good-natured, she recalled, but obstinate and willful at times. Something that for some reason had stuck in her mind with a lingering sense of outrage was a small incident that had happened on a Sunday when she was put in charge of getting her brother dressed up for some important family event. She had managed to get John into his new white

Beth (Mrs. E. G. Ainsworth) with young John. Courtesy of Mrs. E. G. Ainsworth.

sailor suit (an outfit which was all the rage for children in those days), only to discover him, a few moments later, sitting on the edge of the unpaved street in front of the house, playing in the mud, which now covered him from head to toe. I began to realize something that would come to me over and over again during the years of interviewing that lay ahead. The memory has a logic of its own that has much more to do with the emotions of the rememberer than any outside measuring stick of what's important or not important.

I asked her to look back and tell me what this home had felt like in those days. For example, what happened when the family got up on a weekday morning? The gray-haired woman who sat next to me in the car looked out the window through her gold-rimmed spectacles at the house, newly repainted a peculiar mustard color, and answered with short bursts of recollection. They knew it was time to get up, she said, when they heard their father working the tall red coffee grinder in the pantry. He'd check the fire in the stove, and if more wood was needed, he would go down to the basement and stack it on the dumbwaiter and haul it up to the kitchen. About this time, their mother would be down to start the bacon and put on the water for the cereal. She always looked just as if she had stepped right out of a bandbox, completely dressed and perfectly groomed, even the first thing in the morning. When they all went in to sit down for breakfast, there would always be flowers in the center of the table. Their father was very proud to be able to put flowers on the table from his garden any time of year.

Before Mrs. Ainsworth—Elizabeth—and her sister, Esther, were through with the dishes, their father was on his way to the Sperry Flour Mill, where he was the manager. The two girls would join their friends in front of the house for the walk to high school, while John crossed the street to Glenn Graves's house—Mrs. Ainsworth pointed to show me the house—where the two boys, so clean and serious, would start out for the square, brick-walled "Baby School," as the primary school was called, several blocks away. Now that the children were off, their mother would be getting ready for some meeting or other. "She spent an awful lot of time on strangers," Mrs. Ainsworth said with a sigh.

I started up the engine and drove slowly, at Mrs. Ainsworth's direction, through the neighborhood. There was where Johnny Burgess, one of John's childhood friends, had lived, and there was where Dr. Murphy lived. John Murphy used to chase John home from Baby School every day and hit him if he caught him. There was where the Baby School used to stand. "I wonder," Mrs. Ainsworth mused, "if the Murphys are home. You ought to meet him." We drove out to what, over the years, had become the more affluent part of town, replacing the older district of two-story Victorian houses where the Steinbecks had lived. We parked in front of a white Spanish-style ranch house with a bright, beautiful garden and called on the Murphys.

The four of us sat in the dim, cool living room, while John Murphy, with occasional help from his wife, talked about how John Steinbeck had helped their son, Dennis, when he was in despair as an aspiring writer and helped them, too, understand what their son was going through. Then Mr. Murphy began to reminisce about childhood and growing up with John. He remembered the two of them as hell raisers, and Mrs. Ainsworth began to squirm a bit on her chair.

On one occasion, Mr. Murphy recalled, they and another boy, named Elmer Taft, were out in an orchard eating cherries, and finally they had their fill and started a little war, picking green apricots and throwing them at each other. After a time, they got up on the roof of the farmer's barn. The farmer, hearing the ruckus, came out of his house to get after them. The boys started to escape so quickly that the Taft boy fell off the barn, knocking the wind out of himself. He was in terrible shape, but the two Johns refused to leave their wounded and managed to pull and half-carry him out of the orchard to the nearby Murphy home. Murphy's father was the Steinbeck family doctor, and the boys sneaked into his office.

They had tried for several minutes to get the boy to recover, but he was still dazed and out of his head, so John

Steinbeck suggested they go into the office to look for some medicine to make Elmer feel better. Whiskey seemed like a good bet, and they found some in a cabinet. To bring the boy to, they kept pouring whiskey down his throat. And Elmer kept choking and throwing it back up, along with the cherries. At last, after losing a lot of whiskey, they picked up the boy and carried him home. This took a lot of courage since by now he smelled very bad. They propped Elmer up against the porch siding and knocked on the door. When the poor boy's father came, they said, "Here, Mr. Taft, here's your son," and then they ran like hell.

It was a marvelous story. Although it had obviously been perfected and polished over the years, I later found confirmation of it in one of John's letters to a third party. But when I got into the biography business and was working on the manuscript, I found I couldn't use it. I found the hardest portion of a life to write is the childhood. Everyone remembers stories that to them are somehow typical, in a Tom Sawyerish way, of a young boy, and if I used them, I would end up with a kind of Norman Rockwell cartoon of John Steinbeck's early years that could be entitled "Boys Will Be Boys."

Mrs. Ainsworth laughed but was clearly uncomfortable. I was to find over the years that, as candid as she wanted to be—and I've run into few people as forthright—her sore spot was the subject of John in any connection with liquor. At the end of our last interview together, she asked if I would please not give too much emphasis to John's drinking. She was not herself a teetotaler—we had had a glass of wine together on several occasions—but she did seem to be worried about the effect of John's drinking on his sons, that my discussion of it might harm them. She did not know what I would find out later, that the two boys had, while growing up, witnessed any number of horrendous drinking scenes and were quite beyond being touched by anything as trivial as the mention of drinking in my book.

By this time, I had swung to the opinion that I should do a biography. Mrs. Ainsworth had introduced me to a number of people who had known John, and the opportunity presented to me seemed too good to pass up. But what kind of biography—a critical biography, an interpretative biography, a thematic biography—was not at all clear to me. Elizabeth had written to John's widow, Elaine Steinbeck, and I was invited to go to New York to meet her. This would be a sort of final test for me, although I was unaware of it at the time.

I did not relish the trip for several reasons. For one thing, we were nearly broke, and such a trip is expensive. For another, I had had only one previous experience in New York, and it had been unpleasant. In the winter of 1965, I was just finishing writing my Ph.D. dissertation and looking forward to getting a job in a four-year college or university. It was almost mandatory in those days that, to arrange for such a job, one had to attend the annual meeting of the Modern Language Association, the major professional organization for college teachers of English and foreign languages. My wife, Sue, and I landed at Kennedy and made the mistake of taking a taxi into the city. The fare was $13.50, a lot of money to us, and I gave the driver a $1.50 tip. He complained bitterly, asked for more, and, when I refused, called me a cheapskate and went into a tirade about outlanders who came into the city expecting to get something for nothing.

Our room in a midtown hotel, for all its expense, was a disaster. It was small, dark, and cramped, and we couldn't turn the heat off. That night it snowed outside, and a freezing wind was blowing up a gale. But even with our windows wide open, it was so hot in the room that we couldn't cover ourselves with the sheet but had to try to sleep naked and uncovered on the bed. I remember lying in bed, looking at the glow of lights from the street shining through the window onto the ceiling, listening to the almost continuous wailing of sirens, wondering what we had gotten ourselves into.

Before coming, I had written seventy letters to various schools asking for interviews. I had received four affir-

mative replies, only one of which seemed to reveal any enthusiasm. When I called to confirm my appointments, two
of the interviewers had decided not to see me after all. My
first interview of those remaining was with a midwestern
university that offered a one-year, temporary appointment
to teach four sections of freshman composition at a salary
below anything I had ever heard of (I had begun teaching at
a California junior college several years earlier at $2,900 a
year). The second appointment was with the representative
of a well-known, but not elite, eastern university. All my
hopes rested here, for this was the school that seemed to
be really interested in me. However, I had been in the
room for only a couple of minutes, barely having said hello,
when there was a knock on the door, and a second candi-
date entered. He was asked to join us, and from that moment on, the interviewer devoted his attention solely to
the newcomer. I squirmed in my seat for a few minutes and
then got up. The department head barely acknowledged
my leaving.

Returning to my room, I began in desperation to call just
about every chair of an English department listed in the
convention directory. I hadn't written to Harvard and similar schools, but after being turned down by everyone else,
I figured I had nothing to lose. Like most other people, I
am very bashful about calling up strangers (a great disad-
vantage, I would find, to the biographer), and so I found
the process painful, but I called and called, and was refused
and rebuffed by the voices of tired men and women who
were sorry that they had answered the phone. Then I
called the chair of the department at the University of Chicago, Gwin J. Kolb. When he told me that he was not
hiring that year, I asked him if I could just come and meet
him, since I had come all the way to New York and hadn't
been able even to talk to anyone. He surprised me by inviting me to come to his room.

I was greeted at the door by a tall, bespectacled man
who, with a very quiet manner, asked me to sit down and
tell him a little bit about myself. Professor Kolb is very per-

ceptive. I had not spoken more than a few sentences before
he knew that, although I had spent more than a decade in
graduate schools, I had no idea whatever of what academe
was or how it worked. First of all, he told me, you are too
old—thirty-five. Universities are looking for young, promising people who have gone straight through to their doctorate and who can be highly recommended by their faculty
adviser to friends in departments in other universities.
How about my experience? I protested. Doesn't that count
for something? I have many recommendations.

No, he said, your experience in a junior college will
count very much against you. Many universities look down
on junior colleges as being at the bottom of the academic
ladder, and they suspect that anyone who has spent much
time in such an institution will not have the scholarly approach to his work that they prefer. Have you published
anything?

No, I said. I have been teaching a full load and getting
my Ph.D. at the same time. Then, he said, you must do so,
if you want to have any chance of a university job. I started
late myself, he added, and I have been running to catch up
ever since. If you want such a job, you must start to run
also. I knew that he spoke the truth, for in the hallways of
the conference, I had seen the graduate adviser from the
university where I was getting my degree shepherding two
graduate students ten years my junior, introducing them in
animated conversation to chairpersons and the powers that
be, while very deliberately ignoring my presence.

I was grateful for Kolb's advice but felt terribly deflated.
I was so proud of being what I thought was a good teacher,
and now it appeared that I had not done any of the right
things at the right times. Nevertheless, I was able to get a
job the following spring—which surprised me—and to get
it largely on the basis of my teaching record. San Diego
State, which has a reputation as the most scholarly and
most devoted to research of the California state universities, hired me not for my promise as a scholar but as a
supervisor of student teachers training to teach English in

high school. Still, I went ahead on Professor Kolb's advice, and in the next four years I wrote a book on Hemingway, drawn from the research for my dissertation, and also published a couple of articles.

These, then, were the impressive credentials that I brought with me to New York and to Mrs. John Steinbeck for the most important interview, or series of interviews, of my life. If you were the widow of one of the most famous writers of our time, would you pick this man to do his biography?

1

In the Big City

Since I had been in New York before, I was determined to be a wise traveler and take a bus into town from the airport, rather than a taxi. I had some trouble finding the bus stop but finally got aboard a bus with all my luggage, and we headed out, but not on the expressway as I expected. Instead we took a route around the airport to a nearby hotel. I was beginning to get worried. If I hadn't been so bashful and afraid of appearing stupid in the big city, I would have dashed to the front of the bus and demanded to know from the bus driver where we were going. But I was certain that the sign on the front of the bus had said something like "Downtown," and so I settled back to wait it out, trying to convince myself that I had gotten on a "local" that made stops on the way into town, rather than an express bus.

Almost an hour later the bus, which had been running for several minutes on the streets in a residential area, stopped, and the driver yelled out, "End of the line!" I had no idea where I was and asked the man who was moving up the aisle in front of me. He looked at me as I was afraid he might look at me and said, "Jamaica." As I got off, I asked the driver how I could get to Manhattan, and he pointed vaguely off in the distance and said, "You get a bus over there."

It was getting dark as I stood on a street corner somewhere in the eastern part of the United States, a heavy suitcase in each hand and a typewriter case under one arm, all dressed up in my one suit and a California-weight overcoat, surrounded by very unfriendly-looking black people. Relations between the races that year were even worse than usual, and it came to me suddenly to wonder, to even care for the first time, Is this the way a black feels when he walks in my neighborhood? I really didn't know which way to go, but I started off anyway, looking for a bus stop. Now and then I passed by groups of young men, who looked very tough, and as they stared—probably in disbelief—at me, I was certain that every moment would be my last.

Every few steps I had to put down my load and rest my arms. It was now very dark, even with the street lights on, and not a store or gas station in sight, just row upon row of dark houses. I was afraid to ask passersby for directions, and the longer I walked, the fewer people I saw, until suddenly it seemed that the sidewalks were deserted.

After a time, I saw a glow of lights off to the left, and so I made my way in that direction—half a block and rest, half a block and rest. When I got to where the bright lights were, I saw that by some miracle I had made my way to a subway station. With great relief, I went down the stairs to the platform, found a map of the system, and after a short wait, got on the right train.

When at last I was able to sit down, surrounded by my baggage, in a half-empty subway car, I found myself staring across the aisle at a grotesque face framed by disheveled hair—a woman who appeared to be a sort of Puerto Rican shopping-bag lady. Something about me seemed to upset her mightily, for she began muttering and grunting vehemently to herself, every now and then staring wildly at me with fierce eyes.

Then, as her fury rose, she began shaking her finger at me, lecturing to me about something in Spanish. So great was her emotion that I did not think it impossible that she might become violent, and I had a vision of her quickly snatching a pair of scissors out of one of her bags and lunging at me across the car with a wild noise in her throat. I received only mild consolation from noting that no one else seemed to take her seriously—here and there about the car were white, brown, black people who paid her not the

John and Elaine Scott before their marriage, December, 1949. Courtesy of Max Wagner.

slightest bit of attention. Next to me, a stocky black man in pea jacket and stocking cap slept through the whole thing.

When I finally got to my hotel, I double-locked the door of my room with a sense of deliverance impossible to describe, and I turned on the Johnny Carson show to check if the real world was still there. It wasn't until the next morning that it came to me as a rather peculiar thing to do—to check on reality by turning on the television.

I spent two days in the city, visiting the New York Public Library and screwing up my courage for further travel. Early the third morning I went to Grand Central Station and got on the train to Sag Harbor, a small seacoast town near the top of Long Island where the Steinbecks had their summer home and where I would meet Elaine Steinbeck, John's widow. As I rode on the Long Island Railroad, I found that all the jokes I had heard about it were true. We

went for fifteen minutes and then stopped and waited for
fifteen minutes. This went on for the entire trip, except
for one wait which was nearly a half hour long. More disturbing than the wait itself was that you never knew why.
Thinking about Mrs. Steinbeck waiting for me at the station, I began to squirm in my seat and fidget with my briefcase. Fortunately, she had had enough experience with the
railroad to judge just about how late I would arrive.

As I came face to face with the Nobel Prize winner's
widow, I was taken aback by how attractive and young-
looking she was. This threw me off immediately, since I had
been expecting someone who was at least approaching old
age. She was also charming and very capable, just how capable didn't dawn on me until some time later when I had
a chance to think back on the trip. I realized then that
she had made detailed plans for my visit. Long before she
married John, she had been stage manager on Broadway for
Rodgers and Hammerstein, and John used to call her his
stage manager whenever he thought she was bossing him
around too much (if she heard me say that, she would say,
"Are you joking? No one in this world could make that man
do anything he didn't want to do"). Well, she stage-managed
my visit so well I didn't even realize she was doing it—a
testimony to her skill or my denseness. Actually, she had
taken so much trouble for me, planning for me to meet a
great many people and to see all that I should see, that if I
had been aware of her great effort, I probably would have
been paralyzed with gratitude.

As it was, I didn't perform very well, take advantage of all
my opportunities. I hadn't been working on the project as
biography long enough to be able to understand the full significance of what I was seeing or to ask the right questions.
And I am not an aggressive, investigative-reporter type. I
dropped the ball quite a lot.

In just a few days Elaine managed one way or another to
introduce me to just about everybody that John had been
close to in town. We had lunch with one person, dropped

in to see another in one of John's favorite haunts, and had dinner (Elaine cooked John's recipe for cioppino) with an Italian-American family that John had loved and had fun with. We stopped by one afternoon to meet the owner of the local liquor store, and he told me about the time that he had found a very old and rare bottle of rum, which he sold to John. John insisted on opening the bottle there in the store and giving the first drink to him. It was a nice story, but I didn't know what to say or ask ("Did he pay his bills on time?" "What liquor did John order most?").

Then we stopped by a boatyard on the harbor to see one of the owners, Dick Olmstead. Elaine warned me that Dick might be a little reticent, and as soon as she introduced us, she found an excuse to leave us alone together. Dick was a pleasant but quiet man, and I am very shy when I first meet someone, so our conversation went something like this:

Jack: "It's good of you to take the time to talk to me."
Dick: "Oh, no trouble."
Jack: "So you knew Steinbeck pretty well?"
Dick: "Yeah."
Jack: "For a long time?"
Dick: "Yeah. A long time."
Jack: "What was he like?"
Dick: "Oh, he was a real nice guy."
Jack: "What did you do . . . when would you happen to see him?"
Dick: "Well, . . . I'd see him around, you know. And then we went fishing together a few times."
Jack: "Did anything unusual or funny ever happen when you were out fishing?"
Dick: "Oh, no. Just the usual stuff, you know."

But even more painful to recall than such occasions of ineptness as this was that Elaine had gone out of her way to arrange it so that I would meet most of the people that had in some way contributed to the characters in *The Winter of Our Discontent,* but I didn't even realize it at the time. I had had the rare opportunity of seeing, at least in part, how a novelist used and combined the materials of his surroundings to create a world, and I had missed it.

Somewhat more profitable to me were the many long conversation-interviews I had with Elaine over a period of several days. I had worked long hours before my trip east to prepare, but it didn't take very long for me to realize that I still didn't know enough to ask the right questions. Nevertheless, with Elaine's help, not only with the answers but occasionally with the questions, I managed to learn for the first time a good deal about the man himself—as distinguished from the facts about the man that I had mastered.

As a guide for our discussion, I followed a chronology, made up of dates from reference works and newspaper clippings, of the years Elaine and John had been together, and I asked about periods for which I had no information. Where were they living, or were they traveling? What writing was John working on? What friends did they see, and what activities were they engaged in? Although I was just getting to know Elaine and was somewhat intimidated by her presence of mind and efficiency, I forced myself to probe a bit, occasionally asking about subjects I thought might be difficult or painful. She was frank but somewhat guarded in her discussion of their problems with the children—her daughter, Waverly, and his sons, Thom and John. And when I raised the subject, she talked about John's public opposition to McCarthyism and the House Un-American Activities Committee, but when I asked about John's relations with Elia Kazan, the Broadway director and novelist, during the time Kazan aroused a great controversy by deciding to testify before the House committee, she simply said, "I prefer not to talk about that."

Then there were a number of painful questions to ask about the decline in the quality of John's writing during the last decades of his life. We talked about *East of Eden* and John's hopes for it in response to the pressure to produce another *Grapes of Wrath:*

Jack: "So after years of planning and a very difficult period of composition, here it was—the big novel."
Elaine: "Elizabeth [Elizabeth Otis, John's literary agent] and I still think it is."
Jack: "Yes."
Elaine: "I think John to some extent . . . I think John thought so too. He enjoyed writing *East of Eden*, and he put—this is a cliché—so much of himself into it. I think in the time I was with him, I feel that this was the book that gave him the most satisfaction."

I told her I'd like to go back and read the novel again, now that I knew more about the circumstances of its composition and how her husband felt about it.

Elaine: "Have you ever read the book in conjunction with the *Journal* [*of a Novel*]?"
Jack: "No, I haven't."
Elaine: "You don't know how many people—strangers—have written me that they have done that. Isn't that interesting?"
Jack: "I've read the *Journal* and read the book and then read the *Journal* again, but I've never tried to do the two at the same time."
Elaine: "I never have either. I'm not sure that I could."

I went on to the related subject of John's journalism during the period of their marriage. I pointed out that earlier in his career he was very jealous of his reputation, often burning things that did not meet his standards. There was, for example, the famous letter to Elizabeth Otis and Pat Covici, his editor and publisher, where he announced that he was going to burn the first draft of *The Grapes of Wrath*. For the first two-thirds of his career, he threw away thwarted manuscripts, and over and over in his letters he said things like, "I'm simply not going to sell out just for money." Yet in the 1950s he began writing what Peter Lisca (with some exaggeration) called third-rate popular journalism.

Jack: "Didn't he know that such writing would be compromising to his more serious work? Or did he separate them in his mind, saying to himself, 'Well, this is one thing and this is something else, and people shouldn't bring the two together'?"

Elaine: "No, I don't think he separated them. I think . . . I have to be very definite about this. I think that as John became successful and found a happy life with me—and John was very content in Sag Harbor—I think he felt . . . I think what happened is that he lost touch, and he simply ran out of things to write about. And I think that *Travels with Charley* was the major attempt to get back. Well, he writes, as a matter of fact, he must get to know his country again. He must go as anonymously as possible. He must go alone. He wrote that . . . I think John wanted to write. I think he wanted to travel. As I said to you, it doesn't bother me very much when it is said of him that his career declined at the end. That happens a lot of times to writers anyway. What I feel so strongly—I said this to you, but I have never recorded it—is that there is more to a man than a writer, than being a writer."

Jack: "Yes, indeed."

Elaine: "That a man has to be all kinds of things: a husband, a father, a private citizen. He has to do the things that he enjoys a great deal: work out here, boating, travel. And I feel that John, the last years of his life, that he became a full man. It is very unfortunate for the literary world that his writing became less for him, but I think that he lived a fuller life in one way because it did. Now he wanted to write. He would want to travel, and he wanted to write. He wanted to have both worlds. To move where he wanted to move and still write . . . and journalism supplied that."

Sometimes we talked in the sitting room, and sometimes it was pleasant enough to move outside to the terrace. The Sag Harbor house is a peculiar one. At the center of it is what was and should be a living room, but even with a large stone fireplace, its vaulted ceiling and cold floor make it al-

The back of the Sag Harbor house, overlooking the terrace and the pool. Photograph by the author.

most impossible to heat. So this, the biggest of the rooms, has been largely abandoned (made into a combination game room, library, and central hallway), and a little sitting room was added, at one end of the house, onto the kitchen. It was in this room—furnished modestly with a convertible couch, easy chair, and TV, and arranged so one could look over a dividing bar into the kitchen—that Steinbeck felt most at home during the last years of his life—a bit strange, considering his fame and wealth.

But it was the land itself, of course, that was the main charm and attraction of the place—a wedge-shaped bluff that stuck out into and overlooked the cove. As one walked out the French doors at the back side of the house, he first encountered a brick terrace, then grass, then a swimming pool set into the grass, then more grass sloping down toward the point and John's little six-sided writing house,

"Joyous Garde." Over all, making it a beautiful park, tow-ered English oak trees.

With us, whether Elaine and I sat inside or on lawn chairs on the terrace, was always Angel, Steinbeck's last dog. Charley, really Elaine's dog, was long dead, and to re-place him, John had acquired a white bull terrier. This was long before the time that such dogs became macho symbols and began being used as guard dogs by urban apartment dwellers. Angel seemed to me the sweetest, best-behaved dog I had ever met. For hours he sat by my side, as I talked to Steinbeck's widow, ever so often gently nuzzling my hand and asking to be petted.

Of all the things I encountered during my trip, I was most impressed by that dog. And I think, when I returned to my wife and family, that was all I could talk about. We had thought about getting a dog, and now I was convinced, and tried to convince my family, that we should get a bull terrier. A few weeks later, we saw an ad in the paper that a litter was for sale. We got into the VW bus and drove to the house, where a jolly, and somewhat dubious, bald-headed man led us downstairs into a spacious basement room which was apparently the dog nursery.

At the other end of the room, about thirty feet away, were the mother and children, looking like little fat pigs. At our end of the room stood the owner, my wife and I, and our two little girls, dressed up in starched print dresses, white shoes, and gloves. The girls stepped forward and stretched out their arms. The puppies responded with squeals of joy and with incredible speed launched them-selves at the girls. They looked something like flying bowl-ing balls as they hit both girls, simultaneously, in the stom-ach, knocking them both to the floor. The girls were too surprised or had too much wind knocked out of them to cry, but just lay there, stunned, while the puppies licked them all over, from head to toe.

I thought at least the last part was a pretty good demon-stration of how affectionate these dogs could be, but my

wife was totally unconvinced that this was the breed for our
family. Eventually, we wound up with a slightly neurotic
Dalmatian.

Before I left Sag Harbor, Elaine made up her mind about
me and gave me her authorization. I had not asked for
that; indeed, I wasn't quite sure what it meant. It was another example of how she had thought the whole situation
through, and I had not. Knowing, in retrospect, how thorough she is, I wouldn't be surprised if she had talked to
Mary Hemingway (who was a friend) or other literary heirs
about their experiences with biographers. I knew that she
was giving me a pledge to cooperate with my work, but I
really wasn't aware at the time of how valuable that can be.
Nor was I aware of the possible disadvantages of authorization. A typical arrangement is one in which cooperation is
given to the biographer in return for approval of the manuscript by the heir. This can turn into a very unpleasant
situation for the biographer if the heir decides he or she
wants to censor those parts of the manuscript that might reflect unfavorably on the subject or on him or her. The biographer is forced, then, to become an accomplice to a form
of dishonesty, and that, of course, can destroy his reputation as a scholar and his credibility.

Unfortunately, because of my naïveté, we did not talk
about these things in detail as part of any kind of agreement. However, Mrs. Steinbeck did talk about her attitude
toward the book, and I talked to her about certain basic criteria that I had developed in regard to it. Fortunately for
me and the project, and a key, really, to whatever success
the book has had as a believable document, Elaine's attitude was that nothing negative about John should be held
back in some misguided attempt to protect his reputation.
This book should be, she felt, totally honest. For my part, I
told her that, while I had sympathy and great interest in
her husband's life and work, I must be very careful to be
as objective as possible and avoid giving any impression

of what the critics had come to call "bardolatry" (having adapted the word to mean the uncritical adulation of any writer, not just Skakespeare). I also tried to convey, as diplomatically as possible, my sense that I needed to be completely independent, which I felt she agreed to.

If I were to do it all again, write another authorized biography, I would be much more specific, even putting some kind of agreement in writing. Although an heir, to cooperate effectively, must put in a good deal of time and, no doubt, pay an emotional price as well, the biographer must spend an enormous part of his life and a lot of money to complete such a project. A commercial biographer can come into a situation and in a few months, without doing any real research, skim off the cream of easily available material and make money, but to do the kind of definitive work that authorization implied required a far deeper commitment. Near the end of my work, my wife and I sat down and figured up what our out-of pocket expenses had been over fifteen years, and the total shocked us.

So I was committing not only my own time and energy, but the family resources to a project, the rules of which I only vaguely understood. I could have easily met disaster if at the end of it all I had run into the kind of censorship or interference that would have forced me to abandon the book before publication. But I was very lucky in that my literary heir, Mrs. Steinbeck, never once suggested, let alone tried to force, any changes in my account of her husband.

I never had time to think about it, so never asked, but looking back I have wondered, Why me? Why was I chosen? Surely there were many well-known and accomplished scholars and writers who would have leaped at the opportunity of doing such a book. Why an unknown like me? I will always wonder, Was it because I was fresh and capable and honest, or because it seemed to those close to Steinbeck, such as Elizabeth Otis, who were determined to protect him, that such a scholar as I, naïve and agreeable,

might be more easily manipulated? I don't think I was manipulated by anyone. But sometimes I wonder.

Events were passing very rapidly, and I felt I needed time
to sit and think things through. However, I believed I must
take full advantage of my presence in New York—air fares
across the country were enormously expensive during that
period—and so I made arrangements to spend another
week in the city. Elaine had provided me a list of John's
friends in Manhattan, along with their unlisted phone numbers, and I selected a few that I would try to see before
leaving for home.

In contrast to my previous experiences in Jamaica and on
the subway, I now found myself intimidated by wealth,
rather than poverty, as I interviewed Steinbeck's business
associates (producers, directors, publishers), friends, and
acquaintances in lavish office suites or apartments high up
in tall buildings. There was something dizzying and dis-
locating in walking or half-running (I was determined to
avoid all forms of transportation in Manhattan for a time)
from one place to another in a strange city and then zoom-
ing up, breathlessly, in rocketlike elevators to be suddenly
delivered into the hands of the wealthy, the influential, and
the famous.

It was a ritual at that time to welcome a visitor with a
drink, and out of politeness I would accept, sipping the
generously provided three or four fingers of Scotch or bour-
bon—rapidly, to match the pace of my schedule. Then I
would find myself down on the street, my briefcase clutched
in my hand, wondering where I was. What street was this?
Which way was uptown or downtown? How would I get to
my next appointment, and once I got there, would I be co-
herent? After several experiences of this kind, I determined to risk offending my hosts and decline all offers of
strong drink.

On the streets of midtown, I couldn't help noticing that
every block, or even half block, there was a policeman

standing, and in every store, even the smallest grocery or
delicatessen there was a security cop. I did not find this reassuring. I began to worry that someone might snatch my
briefcase, and so I complicated my schedule by dashing back
to my hotel every chance I got to deposit my interview
tapes in the hotel safe. Every time I saw a policeman on
a corner, I would reach down and touch the bulge of my
traveler's checks in my pants pocket. It became a sort of tic,
fingering my left thigh, as I raced up and down Manhattan streets, brown-plaid overcoat flapping in the wind behind me.

To make as much time as possible, I followed the advice
in one of Steinbeck's letters. He had discovered that if you
try to look in people's faces as you approach them on a
crowded city sidewalk, they will walk right over you, but if
you look down at the pavement, they will get out of your
way. I tried it, and it worked—an immediate practical ap-
plication from the study of literature.

As a middle-class boy out of the western provinces, I had
had no experience with the people of wealth and fame that
I was suddenly exposed to. As I sat in one beautifully decorated living room after another, my senses began to reel
from the overload. One penthouse was like a beautiful old
Spanish-style cottage, with exposed beams and what appeared to be stuccoed adobe. The inside and the garden outside flowed together with an abundance of plants. It was
hard to remember that all of this was on top of a tall building.

Another penthouse took my breath away. The living
room was as big as our whole house, and we could not have
furnished it—just in terms of the quantity required to fill
such space—with the savings of a lifetime. A matched pair
of sleek English setters of a strawberry-blonde color romped
up and down hallways that seemed to run half the distance
of a football field. Overlooking Central Park, the living
room, with its floor-to-ceiling window, seemed to blend
into the park below—a rug had been custom-woven to
match exactly the colors of the treetops.

2

Lost in High Tech

When I wasn't shopping, taking the girls to school, picking them up from girl scout meetings, or working on the house or in the yard, I was trying to grab every minute I could from my normal work load of correcting papers and preparing for classes so that I could do the background research for the biography. This was usually a couple of hours in the afternoon and from after dinner for as long as I could stay awake. In addition, I tried to get as much time in the university library as possible, since much of the material I was concerned with was noncirculating and had to be used in the library.

The background research I needed to do, before I even ventured out to consult unpublished primary materials— letters, journals, and manuscripts—consisted of reading everything I could get hold of locally which had been published by Steinbeck and about him. John had been a relatively prolific writer, and he had been popular and controversial enough that much had been written about him both in the popular press and in academic journals. So, all in all, even the preliminary work was formidable.

By contrast with my graduate training days, twenty-five years ago, when all you needed for research was a pad, a pencil, and a resilient bottom, the process today is far more complex, requiring that the researcher learn how to deal with a variety of machines and electronic devices and, what is sometimes more difficult, the rules and customs surrounding their use. People somehow related to literature, such as writers, scholars, and librarians, often seem ill at ease in dealing with anything mechanical, but out of the necessities of early poverty I had learned to fix a car or a washing machine and how to plumb or wire a house. My pride in this, however, was humbled, and as far as my tenure as a biographer was concerned, I might as well have been a mechanical dumbbell.

My attitude toward interviewing equipment was that I should get the best available. The most expensive cassette recorder didn't cost one-tenth what it cost to fly to New York and stay a week. I decided also to buy the best tapes available. It took me many months after I started interviewing before I could find someone to transcribe them, and by that time I had recorded a number of tapes. The woman I found to do them did excellent work but had all kinds of trouble with the tapes sticking in the tape player.

At first we thought it was the playback-transcription machine (a special tape recorder fitted with foot pedal and a segment reverse), and I took the machine in several times to be serviced. When the problem continued (she was spending more time trying to get the tape to play than in transcribing), we tried her home stereo tape deck, then my original recorder, and finally a rented transcription machine. After months of struggling with the problem, nothing seemed to improve it. I couldn't believe it, but it occurred to me that something was wrong with the cassettes.

I consulted the dealer, who referred me to the West Coast representative of one of the largest tape manufacturers in the world. He confirmed my suspicion on the phone that there was indeed something wrong with the super-deluxe, super-expensive tapes I had purchased so as to avoid any possibility of trouble. Thousands of the cassettes had been manufactured with a case a millimeter too small, so that in playback they bound up and stuck. So much for the axiom of paying top price to ensure quality. By the time I found what was wrong, I had nearly fifty recorded tapes from interviews all around the country. The factory representative generously offered to replace all my tapes without charge.

Over the next year we struggled with the tapes, putting the most stubborn ones into new cases and forcing others, a few inches at a time, through the machine. I searched for a lesson in all this, as teachers of literature are wont to do, but the only one I could come up with was to test things out thoroughly before going too far with them. But this guide to future conduct did not save me from other similar disasters.

Once I was committed to do a biography, rather than just a critique of Steinbeck's work, I was forced to add other tasks to my preliminary research load. The main task was to establish a basic chronology. I decided to ignore, for the most part, the chronologies that had already been published and start fresh with my own. The early years I would have to cover later by referring to the Salinas newspaper, county records, and school transcripts, but I could cover in my own university library the years from the time John achieved fame in the mid-1930s to the end of his life. I would need to copy all references to him in news magazines, indexed newspapers, and such other miscellaneous sources as *Facts on File*.

This material was available to me only on microfilm and in those days could be copied only in our university library on a special machine that kept breaking down or running out of supplies. It was a wet-process copier, and copying several items required that the copies be spread out on nearby tables to dry and later stacked with sheets of paper towel between them. In addition to its other shortcomings, the machine was painfully slow, so that copying took hundreds of hours made up of an hour snatched here and there between classes.

A year after I had finished this task, I was ready to begin a permanent filing system and removed the material from its temporary storage to be rearranged and indexed. When I looked inside the folders, I couldn't understand at first what it was I was looking at: copies, paper towels, and in some instances the folders themselves had been reduced to a black, pulpy mass. There was an acid in the process that over time ate through everything. I was devastated and considered for a time giving the whole thing up.

After I recovered somewhat from the loss, I thought about what I should do and decided to try to get the money together to hire a student to repeat the work for me—a remedy I considered only because in the meantime the library had acquired new, dry-copy machines. The work was completed again, this time in only a few months, and I indexed and filed the material. Several years later, when I began the preliminaries for writing the manuscript, I had occasion to go to these documents to cross-check some dates. I opened the first folder, then another, then another. All the pages had faded away and turned completely blank. I still have these copies in my file. After what they cost me, I can't bear to throw them away even though they are meaningless.

The photocopier is far more reliable—although copies made from handwritten script in blue ink can be so dim as to be unreadable, and eventually I had to make and use thousands of pages of copies of John's handwriting from his letters. This machine's availability in most libraries has really revolutionized the research industry in the last couple of decades. What used to take hours or days to copy now takes a few minutes, and what might have taken months before can now be done in a few hours. It can be expensive, as much as fifty cents a page in some instances, but even at that rate, photocopying is a good deal cheaper than staying in a motel for weeks at a time, as I did in Austin, Texas, to take notes and copy passages from Steinbeck's correspondence with his editor, Covici.

In fact, a good deal of my time over the next few years of the early and mid-1970s was taken up with extensive visits at one library or another at various places throughout the country during which I did a lot of hand-copying of materials, sometimes with a guard that seemed to hang over my shoulder in the expectation of some outrage. Usually, however, librarians are very kind to visiting scholars—kindred spirits, really—and in only a few instances did I have unfortunate experiences.

The only library that refused me access to its Steinbeck materials was Columbia University's, even though I had permission from both the literary heir, Mrs. Steinbeck, and the donor of the material, Annie Laurie Williams (who had been John's film and theatrical agent). At the Bancroft Library at the University of California (which in the long run gave me a lot of help), the librarian in charge of the manuscript room had the hatchet face and hawklike eyes of my sixth-grade English teacher. He watched me very carefully for four days. On the fifth day I came back from a lunch break and absentmindedly scooped up from my briefcase a ball-point pen (a forbidden instrument in a manuscript room) along with a half-dozen pencils. This gentleman had made it clear from the beginning that he didn't think much of so-called scholars from the California state universities (by contrast to *the* university at Berkeley), and the appearance of my pen was the breakdown in law and order he had been waiting for. He swooped down on me, and when he was through, I felt just about the same as I had felt back in the sixth grade when I had left my homework at home.

Although photocopiers were usually available, during the early years of my research, I was not very often allowed to use them or to have photocopying done. It was my misfortune to have begun my work at a time when libraries were, for the most part, resisting photocopying, and for good reasons. It is the job of the manuscript librarian to protect the well-being of documents, which can be worn, creased, or defaced in the copying process, even when the copying is done by a trained member of the library staff and not the visiting scholar. But just as important is that these documents have often been purchased for a great deal of money (a handful of letters by a major modern author can sell for twenty or thirty thousand dollars, and a library, such as that at the University of Texas, may spend millions on its collections of materials related to recent British and American writers). And once the documents have been copied, there is no way to halt subsequent copying, so that what was an exclusive possession is now floating around God knows where or among how many people.

University libraries try in various ways to restrict the uses of their photocopies, but none of these really does the job of limiting circulation of their materials, and some measures don't do anything but add difficulty to the job of the researcher. One library did its photocopying on sheets of paper which had the name of the university and "DO NOT DUPLICATE" in large letters all around the margins. This simply meant that I could not read Steinbeck's handwriting at the sides, top, and bottom of the pages because it was obscured by the warnings. I had to guess at nearly every sentence.

Another library would not photocopy but would make a microfilm. Since for my project I could not work from microfilm but had to be able to spread out selected letters and other materials on the desk and tables around me as I wrote (and I was understandably reluctant to use a microfilm copier), I had to type a copy from the microfilm. (I tried to get various typists to do it, but none of them could read Steinbeck's handwriting.) Typing while looking through a microfilm reading machine is not easy to begin with but was very difficult in this case: the outfit that had done the photography was apparently inexperienced, for it had not altered the settings on the camera during the shooting to match the darkness of the ink or paper. As a result, some pictures were overexposed, some were underexposed, and a number of frames were out of focus, and so I had the frustration of having the material in hand but being unable to get at it.

Of course, not all of the documents I needed were at libraries; many were in private hands. I was lucky in that several of these collections, mostly letters, were owned by recipients who had been close friends of Steinbeck and who were concerned that I have access to them so that the best possible biography would be produced. Such was the case with both Webster ("Toby") Street and Carlton ("Dook") Sheffield. I spent almost five weeks in a spare room in Street's law offices taking notes on his letters from John over the years. At the same time I was there, another scholar, Richard Astro, who was doing a book on the Steinbeck–Ed Ricketts friendship, was also working with the letters and interviewing Street. Before I left Monterey that summer, I asked Toby why he was willing to give up so much of his time talking to me, Astro, and many others. He answered, "Because I think it is important that you get it right."

Another recipient of Steinbeck's letters drove me and various members of the Stanford University Library staff crazy. She was a woman who had gone to school with John and who was now in her mid-seventies. She was a pleasant woman, but loquacious and self-centered. She talked willingly about herself at length, but not always in connection with Steinbeck. She had some letters and provided copies for me to use. Mrs. Steinbeck was also interested in using some of the woman's letters in her collection (published in 1975 as *Steinbeck: A Life in Letters*), and Stanford wanted to add her letters to its Steinbeck collection. But the woman tended to lead us all on, first seeming to promise the letters, then changing her mind. I made a number of special visits to northern California just to see her, at her request, because she had written me that she wasn't sure or had changed her mind or wanted to talk it over. This went on for years, back and forth, including several talks with intermediaries who were supposed to, I guess, act as advisers and referees. The same sort of thing was happening to Stanford and to Elaine, and they finally lost patience with her. I held on and finally was able to get from her what she had initially promised to me—partial quotation from several letters.

Part of the problem, at least at the end, was her concern over the possible sale of the letters. I didn't know, but I had the feeling that a manuscripts dealer had gotten hold of her and told her that if I used parts of the letters their value would be significantly decreased. (This usually isn't true. The value depends on what is in the letters and how early or rare they are. Those very letters recently sold for just about the same amount they would have sold for if pieces of them had not appeared in the biography. Sometimes when the importance of a letter is made clear in the context of the life in a biography, the value increases significantly.) All in all, there were about a half-dozen sets of letters I was unable to consult because the recipients were worried about depreciated value.

For this and other reasons, my experiences with dealers during my work on the biography did not make me a fan. They seldom know anything about the materials they are selling, but it seems to be the nature of their business that they must pretend to know everything—thus many of them assume a hauteur that can be matched only by owners of art galleries.

Sometimes it works out that a key document is in the hands of a dealer. Such was the case with the unpublished manuscript of "The Wizard of Maine." This was the unfinished libretto that Steinbeck had written in the 1950s for a projected musical comedy. The idea for the musical had been developed in a brainstorming session with Frank Loesser, and Lynn, Frank's first wife, had described the essence of it to me, but I thought I should see it for myself. There were two versions, both in the hands of dealers, one on the East Coast and one on the West. I called the dealer who was located in Santa Barbara, and he agreed to let me read the manuscript. I was surprised and pleased. I made an appointment for eleven on Saturday morning but drove the two hundred miles the night before, staying at a motel so as to be sure to be on time. The next morning I drove downtown and, in accordance with the dealer's instructions, called him for specific directions to his place of business. He told me on the phone that he was sorry but he had forgotten all about our appointment and had sent the manuscript off to a possible buyer in the Midwest the day before.

The dealer in the East who had a considerable amount of Steinbeck material also made a fine impression on me. One of his assistants wrote with a list of things for me to identify. His approach was not "Would you please" or "If you can find the time, we would appreciate," but simply "Do it." I ignored it. And then there was the dealer in northern California. Near the end of my work on the biography, just before publication, I was trying to clear up the permissions for some letters that I had used. Stanford was not sure whether it had the publication rights, which then could be granted to me, or not. I had to try to trace back the acquisition of the letters to the original source, if possible, and so began with the dealer who had taken the material to the library.

I called him, and he was very curt and impatient on the phone. He made it quite clear in his tone of voice that I was wasting his time. "Who are you?" he kept asking, and I tried to explain I was the authorized biographer, I had a problem, and I needed his help. His response was "Authorized by whom?" I told him that I was authorized by Steinbeck's widow. "Don't you know that Steinbeck had three wives?" he countered. So it had come to this: after fifteen years, thousands of documents read, hundreds of interviews conducted, I was being lectured to by some pompous ass about how many wives John Steinbeck had had.

After Elaine gave me her authorization, one of the first things I wanted to do was spend an extended period of time in the Salinas-Monterey area. I applied for a small grant from the American Philosophical Society and got it. This enabled our family to move up to Salinas for most of the summer of 1971. On a hunch, I wrote to the high school asking if anyone on the faculty wanted to rent his house, and we were able to make arrangements for the house of one of the coaches who went with his family to a second home every summer. So, VW bus packed to the gunnels, including two tricycles and a cat, we moved to Salinas.

The poor cat was traumatized by the move, and our small daughters were confused. They had no experience of city or town life, so when we told them to ride their tricycles only on the sidewalk, we later found them riding up and down the gutter, not ever having seen sidewalks before. Another adjustment we had to make was that we had the false im-

Lettuce fields near Salinas, California. The Santa Lucia Mountains are in the background. Photograph by Richard L. Allman.

pression that many have that Salinas is hot during the summer (I swear that every time I have driven through it in the summer the temperature has been over 100), but it is not. There is often an overcast, or, as we used to say in San Francisco, a "high fog," and in the afternoon a cool wind can actually be chilly. So we brought the wrong clothes. The house itself was something of a disaster area (that was the summer we discovered a cleaner that cuts through everything—even paint, if you are not careful), but we cleaned and arranged as if we were on another camping trip and settled in. The neighbors made us feel welcome, particularly on the side where we had a highway patrolman married to a juvenile probation officer. It was the probation officer who taught my wife how to make a martini with freezer-chilled vodka and three drops of juice from cocktail onions.

For the first couple of weeks I spent much of my time at the Steinbeck Library, the main branch of the public library, going through its collection of clippings, memorabilia, and letters. From my very first day there, the director, John Gross, became my friend and provided a thorough orientation—tips, warnings, local color, and a list of people that I should try to see. I also had from Mrs. Ainsworth a list of people yet to see.

Of all my activities as a biographer, the one I was least fitted for and which caused me the most anxiety was that of interviewer. I do not, as I have said, have a Woodward-Bernstein personality. But the problem was deeper than that. It may have stemmed from one of the worst experiences of my life, which came when I was a young child selling the *Saturday Evening Post* door to door. In those days, a man used to drive up and park near an elementary school. These days he would probably be selling drugs, but at that time he would call out, "Hey, kid! Any of these things you want?" and you would walk up to the open window of the car, look down on the passenger seat, and see all manner of marvelous things laid out on a black-velvet pad. There were penknives and cameras, pen-and-pencil sets and wrist watches. Things to make a young boy, who had no allowance or money to buy things, drool. All you had to do was sell fifty magazines a week for five weeks. Easy enough, you thought.

So you took your bag, which hung from your shoulder and draped down along your side, and your magazines. Every young boy at this point in our history was still being taught that he could do anything if only he tried hard enough. So I tried very hard, going door to door to door. I went through my own neighborhood quickly and then went on, ending up every day after school far from home in one strange neighborhood after another. This was during the Depression, and I quickly found out how tough were the times for most people. The very suggestion of buying a magazine for five cents seemed to evoke rage in the breast of any householder willing to answer his doorbell. There must have been some who answered the door who didn't slam it angrily, but I don't remember them.

Now I had to solicit interviews from people I didn't know, call them on the phone and explain who I was. Once again I had to go knocking on strange doors. It was for me a nerve-wracking experience that I had to force myself to undergo, and during the weeks when I was interviewing several people a day in the Salinas-Monterey area, I carried a bath towel in the car to wipe the perspiration from my face, neck, and hands.

One of the most important interviews I had in those early days did not help improve my self-confidence. As I have mentioned, Steinbeck had been married three times, and his first wife, Carol, had been with him during the 1930s when many of his more important works were written and published, including *Of Mice and Men* and *The Grapes of Wrath*. It was absolutely essential that I talk to her, yet she had always in the past declined to be interviewed. With the help of Mrs. Ainsworth, who had remained on good terms with her after the divorce, I was able to get an appointment. I was aware of Carol's reputation for mercurial temperament, and Elizabeth warned me that she would either chase me off with a shotgun or smother me with kindness. Hoping for the latter, I drove out to Carmel Valley to meet my fate.

I realized later that the interview must have been a great ordeal for her and that she, in turn, was intimidated by me. Not me personally—physically I am not very impressive, and with my rumpled suit and perspiring brow I must have looked like a very unsuccessful life insurance salesman. But she must have been intimidated by the idea of talking to her former husband's biographer. She neither shot at me nor loved me to death but, like some wild animal held at bay, circled me warily, pacing the room while I sat on a couch, dripped moisture on her coffee table, and fumbled

Carol Steinbeck near the swimming pool at the "ranch," near Los Gatos, California, 1941. Courtesy of Richard Albee and the John Steinbeck Library, Salinas, California.

with my briefcase. The animal effect was heightened by long gray hair that swung about like a high school girl's every time she turned. She was a big woman, tall and large-boned, and she had the heavily wrinkled skin of a person who has spent a great deal of time in the sun. I had never seen a woman in her mid-sixties with long hair, and the hair in combination with that very wrinkled, old-looking face, produced an effect that was bizarre. She seemed to have a enormous amount of energy—I don't think she stopped moving or sat down during the three hours we were together.

As a preliminary, I asked her whether she minded if I taped our conversation. She bristled at the suggestion and exclaimed, "Good God, I hate those things! Put that away!" And so we were off to a good start. All things considered, it was not a bad interview. I learned several things that were quite surprising. For one, I learned, contrary to every account that had been published about Steinbeck's life, that he never took a journey with the Okies from Oklahoma to California. This "fact" was so well known that it had become a part of American folklore, and I was rather sorry to see it go.

Another surprise came in regard to Steinbeck's politics. I assumed that he had been, during the 1930s at least, a Marxist or very sympathetic to Marxism. I didn't know whether or not he had been a member of the Communist party, but he was thought to have been by some of the people I had interviewed, and was considered a "Red" by some conservatives not only during the thirties but down to the present. Such old antagonisms were part of the reason that Steinbeck usually has more books in the top ten of banned books in schools and libraries than any other writer.

When I raised with Carol the question of his politics, I was nearly floored when she said that, in looking back, she really thought that he was apolitical. At first I thought she might be trying to protect him, but the more I read and the more people I talked to, the more sense it made to me. There was no doubt that he was sympathetic toward the poor and the dispossessed in our society, but at a time of mass movements, Hitler in Germany and Stalin in Russia, when many in our country thought that the only solution to our economic and social problems was a political one that sacrificed individual freedoms to the power of the state, Steinbeck did not agree.

Letters made it clear that he was disapproving of socialism as early as his first years of college and maintained that disapproval throughout his life. Also very early on he developed the stance of the objective observer, and, as he notes several places in his writings, an observer cannot see clearly things as they are if he is partisan and begins labeling what he sees as "good" or "bad." He took this role very seriously; indeed, one of the reasons that fame upset him so much when it came was that he believed it would eventually rob him of his ability to pass among ordinary people unrecognized and observe them, thus destroying his ability to write. He was that strange combination, a caring man who was also very detached.

Although I learned several important things from Carol during our interview, I was still rather disappointed, blaming myself for not pressing harder and having enough courage to speak up. I was certain that Carol was not the kind of person who admired caution. She, too, seemed to feel deflated, and before I left, in a gesture that suggested that maybe she had thought better of her earlier suspicions, she showed me her swimming pool and bathhouse and offered me an imported beer. Then, after a few minutes of idle conversation, she confided in me in a low voice, "John really hated Salinas, you know." I was so touched by the moment that I lied and said, "No—I didn't know that. That's very surprising."

As I drove away, I thought to myself that I had made a beginning anyway. Perhaps if she would see me again, I could win her confidence over a period of time and gradually work toward the more difficult questions. Oh, I thought, she had some stories, some tales . . . if only I could get her to tell them. Carol had the reputation for having a great sense of humor, and I was ready to laugh. I thirsted to laugh with her.

A few days after the interview, as I learned later, she met Ed Ricketts's sister at the local supermarket. I had interviewed the sister during the same period, and in all inno-

cence she asked Carol, "How did you like being taped by
Professor Benson?" Outraged, Steinbeck's first wife stormed
out of the store, convinced that I had double-crossed her and
secretly taped our conversation. I worked very hard in subsequent months to convince her that I had done no such
thing, but although she did allow a brief follow-up interview, I don't think I ever completely erased her suspicion.

3

The Search for the Early Life

At the heart of the biographer's work, his central problem, lies the difficulty of separating the true from the false. There are those who intentionally deceive him by telling him lies or by withholding information, but they are rare. More often the difficulty is with those whose attitudes or values have unconsciously slanted or distorted what they report.

I found that inaccurate reporters fell into four categories. First were those who distorted the record to make themselves look good. For example, some of the testimony of John's second wife, Gwyndolyn, when it was put in the context of the testimony of others, seemed to me clearly to exaggerate her husband's faults while minimizing her own. But such distortion could also be completely innocent and unconscious, particularly with people who had achieved some celebrity by having been Steinbeck's friend or classmate. Several people in Salinas had become almost professional witnesses, since every time some newspaperman (usually on Steinbeck's birthday) decided to do a story or a student had a term paper or an academic had a book, they were directed to the same people, who were consequently interviewed over and over again.

Usually these people were very eager to please, to maintain their authority. Some would play it by ear, picking up clues from the questions and trying to tell the questioner what he wanted to hear. Others had stories polished over the years by telling and retelling. I felt sorry for one gentleman and a bit guilty for my skepticism. No matter what I asked, he would simply pick up some piece of the story he had already told me and repeat it again, as if I had punched

the fast-forward button on a tape recorder and had stopped
somewhere at random.

Second were those who wanted to tear down Steinbeck
to build up someone else. In this category were some of the
admirers of Ed Ricketts. I found in Monterey that there
were a few people who had come to think of Ed as something close to a saint, a genius who had been callously ex-
ploited by his friend. They were certain that, without Ed,
John Steinbeck had neither ideas nor the talent to express
them. Then there were those who would lower their voices,
as if imparting some very dark secret, and tell me that it
was really Carol "who wrote all those books, you know."

Third were those whose antipathy to Steinbeck led them
to repeat stories that put him in a very negative light. Not
all the negative stories were false, of course, but I did get a
number of apocryphal tales from Salinas folk who obviously
bore him a grudge.

There was the woman, for instance, who seriously reported to me that Steinbeck, after writing *The Grapes of
Wrath*, confided to her husband, who owned a ranch near
Tulare, that he had written the book for money and had
filled it with as much dirt and sensationalism as possible to
make sure that it sold. I knew that Steinbeck was never in
the Central Valley in the years immediately following the
publication of *The Grapes of Wrath*, that he would not be
confiding in a ranch owner, especially in such a way as to
undercut his work, and that he would never say to anyone
that he had written a serious work of fiction for money.

Generally, when I heard such things, I simply let them
pass without comment. It wasn't my job to run around town
defending Steinbeck's honor. In this case, however, the
storyteller was a well-dressed, apparently well-educated
matron, who with great conviction had told her tale—not
for the first time, I was sure—and was believed by all those
present. Since we were in company, I felt I had no choice
but to say, "That's not true," although I was sure that I was
making little more than a symbolic gesture. Shocked for a
moment that anyone would dare contradict her, the woman

recovered her haughty expression and sniffed, "Well, I
don't know. That's what my husband told me." Everyone
then turned to me as if we were engaged in a tennis tourna-
ment. Faced with having to call her husband a liar, I was
willing to let it go at that.

Others, with more noble motives, were actually more of
a threat to my search for the truth than those who were
clearly motivated by hostility. It was my tendency—one I
shared, I would imagine, with most other biographers—to
assume the best until the worst was proved, and so I was to
some extent more open to good news than bad. But I had
enough sense to become suspicious when the news was too
good. One of John's best friends during his later years was
Shirley Fisher, an agent at McIntosh and Otis, Inc., the literary agency which represented the novelist. Shirley was a
very loving and emotional woman who obviously cared
deeply for John, and I liked her immediately, but it became
clear rather quickly that she was prepared to recite every
instance of John's kindness or generosity she had been able
to think of. Every time I saw her she would have a new list
of good deeds.

Then when she read the first section of my manuscript,
which covered childhood and the teenage years, she complained that the impression I had given of John was so
negative that no one would want to continue reading the
book. I countered that if I took out all the unpleasant aspects of his character and behavior during these years no
one would believe the rest of the book, even if he went on
to read it—and rightly so. But she remained unconvinced,
and I think she half-thought that I had set out on some sort
of muckraking expedition.

Although while I was in Salinas that summer I tried to see
everyone I could who had been acquainted with Steinbeck,
I was particularly concerned to uncover as much as possible
about his childhood and adolescence. I knew this would be
a difficult period. I was already aware that as an adult he
demonstrated a complex personality, one with a number of

contradictions. I knew that many of the traits that manifested themselves in the writer should have their roots in the conditions and events of growing up in Salinas. But that growing up was fifty-five, sixty years ago—who would remember? Furthermore, there would not be the letters, journals, or confidences given to friends that we had as guides for understanding the grown man.

Children are too easily categorized, and that worried me. And their thoughts—how do we get at those? Upon reflection it occurred to me that we seldom know what a child is really thinking, possibly because we don't usually ask, or, more probably, because children, in response to the authority that surrounds them, develop secret lives and know enough not to tell us their thoughts even if we were to ask. So for the most part the biographer must depend on clues, indications, and indirect evidence—an accumulation of little things. If there is any direct evidence, in a writer's life, it comes as he writes in retrospect about his own growing up. But the recollections of someone forty or fifty years after the events must also be viewed with skepticism and require some form of corroboration.

In comparison to most of his contemporaries, Steinbeck was a notably unautobiographical writer. What he used from his own experience he changed, combined, and disguised in his writing, perhaps because he was so sensitive about revealing himself, so private. Yet there are a few articles where he talks about himself and, even more revealing of the child, a few places in his fiction that are clearly autobiographical. Clues dropped here and there by the adult Steinbeck among family and close friends confirm that there are pieces of *The Red Pony* and parts of the opening section of *East of Eden* that tell us directly as much about the perceptions or thoughts of a young Steinbeck as we are ever likely to know.

The one trait that stands out from these passages was the young boy's precocious awareness of nature. For most of us when we are young, nature is simply there, a given we learn to cope with. For John, his surroundings had meaning

John (third from the left) as an altar boy, ca. 1912. Courtesy the Valley Guild and the John Steinbeck Library, Salinas.

and emotional connotations. If Jody, in *The Red Pony*, had a special place near a spring where he went to be alone close to nature, then we can connect this to John, who, according to childhood friend Max Wagner, also had secret places out in the countryside where he went to be alone. It was John's Irish mother, according to his sister, who impressed on the boy, from the time that he was an infant, that places have meaning.

There were, according to John's mother, not only special places but places that are good or bad, reassuring or threatening. We see this scheme reflected in *The Red Pony*, where the atmosphere is dominated by the two mountain ranges which run on either side of Steinbeck's long valley. On the one side are the sunny, rounded, reassuring Gabilans, while on the other are the taller, darker Santa Lucias. At one point in the novel, Jody looks up at the taller range, up "at the great mountains where they went piling back, growing darker and more savage until they finished with one jagged ridge, high up against the west. Curious secret mountains. . . . When the sun had gone over the edge in the evening and the mountains were a purple-like despair, then Jody was afraid of them."

This reaction by Jody has always touched me, for by some coincidence I know those mountains. When I was a sophomore in high school, five of us went on a camping trip up behind Jamesburg, a few miles south of Salinas. We climbed over Chews Ridge, hiked across the mountains, and then made our way down into the river canyon. Three days into the trip it started to rain, and it rained like a mountain thunderstorm for twenty-four hours. Our tents blew down, everything we had was water-soaked, and the following morning the temperature dropped to 18 degrees (one of us had a thermometer), and everything—sleeping bags, packs, clothing, shoes, and socks—froze.

It started to snow, and for a long time we couldn't get our boots on. Visibility was getting worse and worse, and the trail was being covered rapidly with snow. But we hiked out, some seventeen miles, stamping our feet as we hiked to keep them from freezing, and then crawled the last two hundred yards, exhausted, up the hill to the Chews Ridge lookout station. As we crawled on our hands and knees, we hit each other, cursed, and cried, afraid that we would give up. One boy didn't even get to the last hill and died in the snow. I know those damn mountains.

While almost all of us can be moved to attach a sense of life or death, joy or misfortune to a particular locale in response to an actual event, few of us as children have the incipient perceptions possessed by the young Steinbeck. These perceptions developed as he became older, so that his connection to earth and growing things became crucial elements in both his personality and his art.

One manifestation of this attachment was that he never was without a garden, even in the most difficult of circumstances. During the time he owned his brownstone in New York, he struggled, with compost and care, against soot-filled air, intemperate weather, and lack of sun (his yard, like Willie Loman's, was surrounded by tall apartment buildings) to raise flowers and vegetables—despite advice from all quarters against it. During his last weeks, when he knew he was dying and was confined to his tower apartment in the city, he planted seeds in pots and flower boxes, with little hope of seeing the full-grown results, just to have something near him, growing.

I remember, while sitting on the terrace behind their house in Sag Harbor, Elaine made a point of mentioning that John was always growing things:

He was always starting something from seeds. He might take a seedling tray in that room and talk to somebody and plant inside the house. One day when he was writing, he was out at the little house [his writing room, "Joyous Garde"] here, and he had some old window frames out there, and I could see he was doing something. This was his garden over here behind the workshop. He had vegetables of all kinds—beautiful vegetables—all that spot between the workshop and the bunkhouse there. It was all garden. It's gone to weed now because I can't keep it up.

Her thoughts drifted away for a moment as she looked at the overgrown garden. I tried to restore her train of thought by asking, "Vegetables?"

Oh, all kinds of vegetables. Salad greens, lettuces, tomatoes, squash, onions, everything. But he always tried a revolutionary way, and it didn't always work. But one day I noticed out by the little house that he had some window sashes, and he was writing a book, and he'd come in every once in a while to get himself a cup of coffee. I said, "What are you doing out there?" And he said, "I'm making a playpen for baby lettuces." He wanted to write, but as he was thinking, he wanted something very close by to do with his hands.

Thinking all of this over now, I wonder whether we can ever know with certainty the full implications, in his emotions and subconscious, of what having a garden meant to John Steinbeck. But since the most commonly used mythic-symbolic structure in his work was the Garden of Eden, we can surmise that there was in his own gardening some sense of connection with the history of man and the processes of nature. Then, too, he probably felt a connection with his parents and a continuity with family tradition, since his father, born of farmers, always had a garden and took great pride in what he was able to grow. Perhaps in always planting something John was bringing a little piece of California and his heritage with him. And I would guess there was also a connection, perhaps not so much a thought as an artistic intuition, between the magic of growing things and the magic of words, and the fertility and vitality of the one might stimulate in him the springing forth of the other.

In his writing, there is always a sense that each man is but a part of a larger physical whole, a perception not uncommon among westerners whose sense of the land, climate, and seasons can be palpable and immediate. Often in his fiction that which is outside man becomes a metaphor for that which is inside. He asks the question, "How does your garden grow?" He was suspicious of attempts by his contemporaries to reproduce in fiction the thinking processes of others, and, like the solitary, private westerner he by nature was, he could not report directly on his own thoughts. Instead, he felt that to get at the inner man he need only observe each man's "garden" and how he tended it.

If John was a loner, as many of his friends and neighbors testified, and very early sensitive to nature, the picture one might build from this is of a shy, withdrawn child, one who—rather typically for a nascent author—would escape into daydreams and books. But that was not quite accurate either. He could be very bossy and assertive, so that if he was shy, he was not timid. A number of stories about him made this clear.

One of his closest childhood friends was Glenn Graves. If you were to start at the Steinbeck house and walk about three-quarters of a mile west to the end of Central Avenue, you would come to the ranch once owned by Glenn's parents. It was there, according to Glenn, that John jumped into the water tank one day for a swim. "Don't you know we water our horses out of that water, and we drink out of that?" asked Mr. Graves (the hierarchy of his concern may say a good deal about Salinas). "Well, you've got a strainer on it, don't you?" replied the boy.

This was told as a funny story, but it portrayed to me a boy who had a lot more cheek than I had at that age. I would never have thought to talk that way to an adult. His comment would seem to support his sister's contention that he was spoiled (he was the only boy of four children) and suggests that he had some consciousness of his own social position, since the Steinbecks were near the top of the pecking order in Salinas and the Graveses were not. But, more to the point, this is but one example of a recurring element of belligerence and arrogance in his character throughout his youth that did not make him very likable and that argues against seeing him too simply as a sensitive victim of a Philistine environment.

The picture of Steinbeck as an adolescent was complicated for me by an already established stereotype. Journalists and biographers had depended on the Salinas High School yearbook, *El Gabilan*, to produce a picture of him as the all-American teenager (the next stage after Tom Sawyer). From the yearbook one does get the impression of a very active, socially successful student. There are pictures of John on the basketball and track teams. He is listed as the senior class president, as a leading member of the cast of the school play, as an officer in the school cadets, and as an associate editor of the yearbook.

But as I began interviewing members of John's class and talked to others who were in high school at the same time as John, I got a very different picture. The men who had been on athletic teams with him, such as Ignatius Cooper (son of the only black family in Salinas at the time) and Bill Black, remembered him as a terrible athlete. He had very little to say in the school play (in later years he claimed he had but one line and managed to muff that), and as "right guide" of the school cadets, he just barely made the officer roster. L. E. Johnson, who took the cadets seriously, looked back on Steinbeck's military career in high school with great scorn—John was, as we used to say in the army, a "screw-up." As for his tenure as senior class president for the second semester, the members of his class I talked to didn't even remember that he had been president and couldn't think how, considering his shyness and lack of popularity, he could have been elected.

My guess (which I didn't put in the biography because I had no direct evidence for it) was that the social position of his parents put some indirect pressure on both the faculty and the students. This is something that probably wouldn't count as much today, but in those days, in a small town and in a school with a graduating class of twenty-four where the Steinbecks knew all the administrators, faculty, and parents, John might well have been pushed ahead beyond his own merits because it was expected that he should take that position. Reluctant and shy, with an inner core of rebellion against high school and all its charades, John was probably a handful for a socially ambitious mother.

John playing with Jiggs in front of the Salinas home, ca. 1918. Courtesy of the Valley Guild and the John Steinbeck Library, Salinas.

As I compared what had been written in the yearbook (all true, but misleading) with what I had been told by classmates (which I took to be substantially accurate, since it came from a number of people, some who looked back at the young Steinbeck with affection and some who didn't), my whole sense of the processes of biography as a search for truth began to wobble a bit. What if I had been doing this book fifty years from now, when all of these people would be dead? I would have had nothing but the written record to depend on and none of the oral testimony to modify or contradict it. Wouldn't I have come up with a very inaccurate picture of Steinbeck as a teenager? What does this say about biographies of figures in the past for whom there is nothing but written evidence?

Putting the pieces together from what I had been told by his contemporaries, I concluded that John had a difficult time of it in high school. One interview that was particularly telling in this regard was with William Black. Black was one of several high school classmates who had moved away from Salinas without leaving any family behind, and I was lucky to get a tip that he was living "somewhere near Santa Barbara." Fortunately, he was in the phone book, and I made arrangements with him to stop by to see him on the way back from one of my many trips to Salinas.

Tall and thin, with gray hair and moustache, he reminded me of William Powell and had something of the same courtly manner. He and his wife had a very tidy new home in a retirement area. Although I don't remember anything specific in the house, I do remember that everything was bright and clean and expensive. He talked gently and quietly about his remembrances of John, and I was delighted to find that he had known him not only in high school but at Stanford and in New York during the mid-1920s. I had been unable up to that time to find anyone who had seen John in New York during the period when he worked on the construction of the New Madison Square Garden and worked for and was fired from the *New York American*.

Black remembered John with affection and some sadness, for, although he did not know him well in high school, he was about the only real friend in his own class that John had. He recalled being invited up to John's room and listening to him read from stories that he had written.

Several years after this interview, I was in the library at ·the University of Texas, reading from a haphazard journal John had written during the time of his composition of *The Grapes of Wrath*, and I suddenly ran across Black's name. After talking to him for several hours, I had come to like Bill Black, and it came to me as something of a shock to see John's bitterness, even snideness, in referring to him twenty-five years later. Bill had been the star athlete, the king of the class, a boy who seemed to have none of the doubts and pains and disappointments that most of us experience during those years. John remembered how jealous he was of Bill's social ease.

Along these lines there was something that Carol had told me during our second interview that stuck in my mind. When John was entering high school, his mother sought to prepare him for the social graces by enrolling him in a dancing class. Against his will, he went, and when he got there, the girls in the class laughed at him because he was wearing large, clumsy boots. This scene and its accompanying emotions of embarrassment and shame apparently came back to him over and over again.

Carol thought it was silly that he should remain bothered by such a trivial thing and told me about it in an offhand way as an example of how eccentric her former husband could be. But I know exactly how he felt. The experience became one of those nightmare moments that most of us have when we are young and terribly self-conscious and come back to haunt us at odd times for the rest of our lives. Fifteen years later, lying in bed trying to go to sleep, we suddenly groan aloud, involuntarily, as the memory of that moment flashes into our minds.

My moment came when I was fourteen and got dressed up, as I had before dressed only to go to church, for my first girl-boy party. I went up to the front door reluctantly, pressed the bell nervously, and found, when the girl who had invited me answered the door, that I was a week early. Her father joined us and, assessing the situation, brought me in and, as if I had been invited for a casual visit, served hot chocolate and cookies to me and the family. But it was one of those situations where the kinder he was, the worse I felt. The father tried to pass off the embarrassment, but his daughter accurately sensed what a boob I was and never spoke to me again.

It was this sense of being outside of things, of being awkward and inadequate, and possibly of being made fun of that I think really is at the core of John's turning against Salinas. Most young people tend to rebel against their parents, and John did some of that. But he genuinely liked his mother and father, and so his primary rebellion was against the community that he grew up in.

Such a wholesale reaction may seem strange but is I think understandable. I think he may have felt about Salinas the way I feel about my high school. There were people he liked in Salinas, as there were people I liked in high school, but my overall impression is of a time in my life when I was confined, subject to standards of approval and popularity that I couldn't meet, and at the mercy of gangs of other students who, through intimidation and disruption, made my life miserable. I still think of some of the members of our class with an active hatred, and it would be a cold day in hell before I would go to a class reunion. John would come back to his home town as a young man and wouldn't have anything to do with many of the people he had grown up with. Some thought it was just part of the strangeness he displayed in high school; others thought that he had got too big for his britches.

John survived, of course, because he held to a vision of his own self-worth as a writer. From the time he was a sophomore in high school, he went through the motions of participating as he was supposed to but retired as often as possible to his room, where he worked on his writing. Salinas, and what it stood for to him emotionally, gradually became part of his geographical metaphor. Characteristic of the white middle class in Salinas and the surrounding area, as we see in such works as *The Long Valley*, are tidy gardens and farms, carefully maintained, enclosed, and uniform. The emotional repression, conformity, and even sterility of such gardeners as Elisa Allen in "The Chrysanthemums," Mary Teller in "The White Quail," and Peter Randall in "The Harness" contrast vividly with the joie de vivre of the lower-class outcasts of *Tortilla Flat*. The gardens of Danny's house and his neighbors are filled with weeds, junk, and broken-down chicken coops. Disgraceful.

4

High Anxiety

At home, my research continued. There came a time, after reading everything I could find by and about Steinbeck in print, that I began to turn to unpublished material, particularly letters. I consulted a Steinbeck bibliography that had been recently published by Tetsumaro Hayashi, a Japanese-American scholar at Ball State University, which listed the holdings of letters at various libraries. The list was disappointingly small, and the value of many of the items seemed dubious (thank-you notes and wish-you-were-here cards). But I began writing to libraries for copies of their letters.

I had gathered several dozen letters through the mail when I began my letter-filing system. (I still have the two folders that comprised that system, stuck in the back of one of my filing cabinets.) The labels on these folders reveal the extent of my naïveté: one reads "Dated Letters—Organized Chronologically" and the other "Undated Letters—Temporarily Organized by Addressee." Remember that there were only two folders. Furthermore, I think I had the idea that somehow I would be able to date all the letters "temporarily organized" and end up with only one file.

It became clear rather soon afterward that my preparations were wholly inadequate—Steinbeck was one of the most prolific letter writers of all time. The letters listed in Hayashi's early bibliography (he has since expanded and updated it) turned out to be but a minute portion of the total actually in libraries and still in private hands.

I would discover that John, for much of his life, enjoyed writing and receiving letters, and he followed a morning ritual of warming up to his serious writing by composing as many as half a dozen, usually to old friends, his agent, his editor, or members of his family, but often "letters to the editor" or public officials. At the height of his fame, he came to dread the mail, as he dreaded any interruption (he hated the phone), but even then, he still, in as yet another contradiction, looked forward to the arrival of the mailman every day and would pace and complain if he was late.

From the letters we have located and the ones we know he destroyed, we can estimate that he wrote between ten and twelve thousand during his lifetime, about two-thirds of which are now in libraries or in the hands of the original recipients or private collectors. John hated the idea of anyone (such as a future biographer) "mucking around" in his private affairs and destroyed most of the letters that were sent to him and several collections of his own letters. Among those he destroyed were some that he had sent to his college friend Carlton Sheffield and almost all the letters to his close friend and confidant Ed Ricketts.

John got his hands on his letters to Sheffield when Sheffield's sister asked him to carry a bundle of them, along with some early stories and poems, from Los Angeles to Palo Alto, where her brother had moved. John persuaded Carlton to let him go through the material, and so one evening they looked it over, page by page, and John managed to toss most of it in the fire, including letters written during periods of his early life about which we have very little information. Even sadder is the loss of the letters to Ricketts, no doubt John's most trusted friend. They were burned when John took charge of the estate after Ed's death. I understand why John burned them and I would do the same, but as a biographer I mourned the loss of invaluable material. There are a lot of "if onlys" in the biography business.

Still, there were huge numbers of letters to locate, read, abstract, and catalog. Generally it is helpful to a biographer to have so many letters: they can not only provide insight into the writer's activities and concerns but also help establish dates and the sequence of events. However, many of

Steinbeck's letters were written in an illegible handwriting—one had to know what was going on at the time to read them. Early in his career his handwriting was illegible because it was so small. I have seen postcards on which he managed to squeeze enough words to fill a typed page (I often typed out "translations" to make the material more accessible).

There are several theories about why he made his handwriting so tiny (sometimes only a sixteenth of an inch high). One is that he was so poor for so long that he needed to save materials. Certainly there were times when he didn't have any paper, as when he was snowbound in the Sierra and had to use the margins of old magazines to write on. Economics may have been part of it, but I think it was also a kind of game to him—he liked to show off, baffle, and confound. And one way he did that was by assuming odd habits for a time.

Later in life his handwriting became larger and larger, but all the letters looked the same. You can't tell an *n* from a *u* or from an *ie*. Reading his letters was often exasperating. I would work for hours on what seemed to be a crucial passage (how could one be sure?) in one of his letters, developing each word, letter by letter. I would use a magnifying glass and then try to guess the word by its location in the sentence and by the number of letters—but you couldn't be sure how many letters there were. Baffled by one word in particular, I would take the letter to my wife, then to each of my daughters, and we would sit around trying to come up with possibilities that would fit. An amusing parlor game under other conditions, perhaps, but I didn't have the time for it. I was surrounded by stacks of letters.

Even more frustrating was that most of his letters, particularly those written during the first half of his life, were undated, and I had to date them from events rather than vice versa. Thus one of the major tools that helps the biographer establish a chronology was denied me. John would scrawl "Tuesday" at the top of the page (or sometimes "Pacific Grove" or "Nov. 5"), and since the letters in most of the collections were out of order, it could be a Tuesday in 1928, 1938, or, if he knew the person long enough, 1958. Since he hated the idea of a biography being written about him, I wonder if he scrawled "Tuesday" on purpose. He had enough perversity to think of something like that.

Letters can be very seductive and even misleading. They are tangible and right in front of you. They seem to speak to you directly from the man himself, and you are likely to forget that writers of letters make mistakes, exaggerate, and forget. That is, a letter is no more reliable than a person speaking in a casual way to us, and a letter, just because it is in writing, is not necessarily "fact." Each letter assumes a relationship between writer and receiver with a number of givens, very few of which we, strangers and readers after the fact, are likely to be aware of. Like a minefield, the dangers of misinterpretation lie everywhere on the page before us.

Furthermore, the number of letters sent to one individual as compared to those sent to another tends to distort the picture of relationships and their relative importance. We are inclined, I think, to give more emphasis to relationships which are documented by a lot of letters. For example, during the first half of the thirties, there are probably more letters to George Albee than to anyone else, and I found that he was constantly being thrust into my narrative by necessity—I often simply had no other source to turn to. Yet Albee was really a very minor friend; John had made him a sort of pen pal, an alter ego that he wrote to as one might write in a diary. Other relationships, those with Ed Ricketts, with Tal and Ritchie Lovejoy, and with Toby Street, were far more important, yet, obviously, since they were on location, John was not writing to them. How do you put this straight? You can't just say that John's friendship with the Lovejoys was an important part of his life. You have to dramatize or demonstrate it. But if you don't have interviews with the Lovejoys or letters to them, how do you gain the proper proportion?

This matter of the proper proportion of relationships is probably the most difficult problem the biographer faces, and there is no easy solution to it. He is constantly being manipulated by the information available to him when he may know that what he can't tell you, because he doesn't have the material, is more important than what he can.

Once you enter into such a project as I had in earnest, and the material begins to accumulate, there comes a time when the full implications hit you. Suddenly, you comprehend the horrendous dimensions of the task ahead and wonder whether any human being could possibly do it. When this comprehension came upon me one morning while I was sitting at my desk, surrounded by stacks of books, folders, clippings, photocopies, and empty iced-tea glasses, I began to get dizzy and felt a large, growing emptiness in the pit of my stomach—a little like the feeling you get when you are looking down from a very tall building and your perverse imagination pushes you to wonder what it would feel like to fall.

I found thereafter that I could never look too far ahead or consider too fully what yet needed to be done or these symptoms would return. Sometimes they would come to me in bed, as thoughts of the future would sneak, unbidden, into my mind. Sometimes overcome, I would mumble aloud, twist, and turn, much to my wife's dismay. How could I explain?

The project could have occupied the full attention of a team of researchers over several years, and there are a few literary scholars around the country who do indeed have teams of graduate assistants paid for by their universities or through grants. There was many a time that I wished for that kind of help, especially when the sheer labor of filing, searching through card catalogs, typing, transcribing, and abstracting seemed to go on and on without promise of reaching an end.

Two things seemed to take the most time. One was looking for things. I had a carefully arranged filing system, a card index of the contents, and a chronological file which was cross-referenced and detailed. Yet it seemed that I never could find what I was looking for. When I was working on the manuscript, I would remember a passage that was perfect for what I was saying, but I couldn't remember where I had seen it. So I would begin looking in my indexes, then in the most likely batches of letters or interview notes, and end up, as I did many times, looking page by page through thousands of pages in my entire collection of materials. Usually I found what I was looking for, but I can recall several occasions when I spent nearly a whole day searching.

Two was writing letters. I would spend two or three mornings a week writing to libraries, to people I wanted to interview, to people I had interviewed to thank them, to agencies, officials, and other scholars to ask questions. In return, once the word got out that I was doing the authorized biography, I began getting inquiries myself.

I didn't mind answering genuine inquiries, but I did object to graduate students who wrote to me expecting me to do their work for them. Some of the letters were very demanding: please type out for me a list of all the articles and books you have found useful; please send me an outline of Steinbeck's life; send me a list of all the people you have interviewed in regard to Steinbeck's work on *The Grapes of Wrath*. Once when I answered a request from a doctoral student by telling him that I just didn't have the time or energy to answer all his questions in detail but would do the best I could, though I had already answered similar questions for a couple of dozen others, he wrote back asking me to make out a list of all the graduate students who had requested information from me.

As the word of my project got about, I also got letters from strangers around the country, some just wishing me luck, some cheering me on because Steinbeck was a favorite of theirs, and others providing tips and leads for research. Help came from all sorts of unexpected directions.

Students in my classes came to me with information—one of my best interviews came out of a lead provided by a student who had a neighbor who had an experience with Steinbeck decades earlier. With a name and address and a county map beside me, I drove out to a semirural area of ragged vacant lots and a scattering of worn and patched frame houses. With some difficulty I found the address, which turned out to be a trailer park hidden behind a high fence. These were not mobile homes but old travel trailers, permanently parked in rows to make up, it was clear by looking at the residents, a sort of retirement community. After asking directions, getting lost, and asking directions again, I finally found myself knocking on the rusting screen door of a mostly silver trailer that sat on concrete blocks. It took several minutes, but a tall, husky man in his late seventies or eighties finally opened the door to invite me in. A white stubble showed on Mr. Kilkenny's face, and he grinned at me while apologizing for the litter. All over the floor were empty beer cans, and a pile of empties in the sink. Where there weren't beer cans, there were books, hundreds and hundreds of paperback books, stacked on the floor against the walls, stacked under and over the bed, stacked even on top of the stove.

Mr. Kilkenny moved a couple of books aside, picked up a can of beer, and settled down in a lounge chair, motioning me to take the lawn chair opposite. He asked me why I was interested in Steinbeck, and I told him that I was writing a book—I figured that would win him over immediately. He then told me about meeting Steinbeck back in the early twenties in a hobo camp in the hills behind Berkeley. Those gathered around the fire were mostly World War I veterans on their way to Oregon to find jobs in the lumber camps. They got to talking, and Steinbeck introduced himself and told them he was a writer. He said that he was looking for good stories and that if anyone had a good "humanistic story" he would pay him for it. Kilkenny told a story about himself in Oregon when he was fourteen, saved from death by exposure and starvation by being given the breast of a nursing farmer's wife. The writer gave Kilkenny some money and told him, "I can use that."

Sixteen years after hearing the story, Steinbeck used it as the basis for his ending to *The Grapes of Wrath*. The whole thing was incredible, and I wondered for a moment if the man in the lounge chair hadn't read the story about the farmer's wife somewhere and extended it into an apocryphal literary anecdote. It seemed entirely likely that he had drunk enough beer over the last few decades that the border between what he had lived and what he had read might have become rather blurred. But there was probably no one else in the world on that day but me who knew that, during the period mentioned by Kilkenny, John Steinbeck, after flunking out of school, had hit the road with a bedroll, ashamed to go home to face his parents. Nor was it common knowledge that Steinbeck on several occasions offered to pay people for their stories. I believed Kilkenny. In his notes, while writing *The Grapes of Wrath*, John had written, just before ending his novel, that he was just about to use the story that he had "saved for so long."

Research leads were provided not only by students but also by friends and neighbors. A family living down the street from us had rented a motor home which broke down while they were vacationing in northern California, and as they were waiting in a Greyhound bus station in Marin County, they learned that the woman sharing the bench with them has been an old friend of Steinbeck's and brought her name and address back to me. A fellow professor was waiting in a dealership customer lounge for her car to be serviced and got to talking about authors with a man who had lived near Steinbeck in Pacific Grove. And so it went, on and on.

It began to appear that, for a shy fellow, Steinbeck had known an extraordinary number of people. On one of my many visits to New York City during these years (I became an experienced traveler and always took the right bus into town), I was invited to a performance of a revival of *Most Happy Fella* by the widow of the composer, Frank Loesser,

and his first wife—who are friends. After the play, we went
out to dinner with the star, Giorgio Tozzi, and his manager.
The manager turned to me, as we were sitting over drinks,
waiting for our steaks, and said, "I hear that you are writing
a book about John Steinbeck."

I said, "Yes, I have been working on it for some time.
One of the problems I'm finding is that, although John professed to hate parties and socializing and often resisted
meeting new people, he turns out to have known just about
every important person in the New York and Hollywood of
his time."

The Manager said, "Yes, well, my mother knew him too."

"Who was your mother?" I asked.

"Ilona Massey," he replied. Good grief, I thought, will it
never end?

Being taken to the musical and out to dinner is but one
example of many kindnesses that people lavished on me, so
that being a biographer also had its rewards. People fed
me, transported me, took me around to meet people, or
called to introduce me on the phone. They lent me letters
and photographs. One weekend while I was in New York, I
flew up to Nantucket, where I stayed for two nights with
Nat and Marge Benchley. Off and on I talked to them together and separately; they showed me around the island,
fed me, and took me to a fancy restaurant where we had a
wine far too good for me to appreciate. Nat (son of Robert
and father of Peter) had been one of John's closest friends
and for a time a neighbor, during the middle and later years
of John's life, and although he is a writer himself and had an
idea that he would like to write a book about John, he freely
gave me his storehouse of memories and anecdotes.

I had a similar experience with Joseph Bryan III, who
had been editor of the *Saturday Evening Post* and a free-
lance writer of articles and, at the time I saw him, had just
published his biography of the Windsors. (To complicate
matters, he had just received his copy of the book and was
deeply angry about it. Apparently a copy editor had taken
it on himself to change all of Bryan's dashes, through the

manuscript, to other marks of punctuation, without clearing the changes with Bryan. This, of course, altered meanings here and there throughout the book. More about copy editors later.)

Bryan was of an old Virginia family and had acquired a beautiful old (really old—about the time of the Revolutionary War, as I remember) house and estate. Bright-green lawns stretched in every direction, lawn more beautiful than I had ever seen except in movies of British ancestral estates. There were columns, of course, under the portico, large rooms with grand high ceilings and imposing doorways, tapestries, paintings, and antique furniture. We were served a delightful French luncheon (Bryan's wife is French) by a maid in uniform, and I hardly dared eat for fear I would do something stupid, like slurp my soup or take up a fork out of order.

Afterward I was invited into a sitting room to look over John's letters to Bryan. While I was doing this, he called his dog in to eat, a fine-looking yellow Labrador bitch, almost platinum-colored. I can see her now in a sort of slow-motion movie in my mind, running with fluid strength in the bright winter sunlight across the acres of rolling, fresh-mowed grass toward the house. Bryan explained how he had had her specially bred and then shipped cross-country. She was an aristocrat, all right, gentle, sharp-eyed, and very well behaved. Bryan waited until I had finished the letters and then gave me his notes. They were the kinds of notes that a writer takes—observations, anecdotes, events, conversations—intending to use them someday as the basis for an article or book. Perhaps Bryan had thought to do his own memoirs, or perhaps a piece about Steinbeck. I didn't know, but I was very touched by the sacrifice.

When our Dalmatian died, we got a yellow Lab, almost platinum-colored. She comes of Scottish stock, with champions back twelve generations on both sides of her family. She, Tess of Glendon, is an aristocrat too, although she lives in San Diego suburbia, her lawn is partly brown most of the time, and she is not quite as well behaved.

After managing to pull myself out of the Slough of Despond, I found my progress endangered once again, this time by encountering Presumption. Almost inevitably, it would seem, the biographer starts to identify with his subject. I knew from the beginning that there were certain superficial similarities between my life and John's. We were both half-German and half-Irish-English, which might explain our work discipline on the one hand and our sentimentality on the other, and both born into middle-class families in northern California. Like his parents, my mother was more socially inclined than my father, a quiet, undemonstrative westerner who had been reared on a northern California farm. About the only social activity that engaged my father or John's was membership in the Masons.

As a child I too had been very fond of the Arthurian legends and had play-acted them with wooden sword, and I suppose that I too had been something of a loner and misfit in high school, a failure as an athlete and too shy to date girls. Like Steinbeck, I had wanted to become a writer as early as my first years in high school and had begun writing in much the same way, with humorous sketches and verse. And I had also gone to Stanford, where, thirty years later, I even had some of the same professors, while taking, like John, courses in English, creative writing, and philosophy. I had no occupational goal in college but, again like John, took largely what interested me. However, I was much more intimidated by the system and conformed well enough to get a degree.

But knowledge of these and other similarities had little effect on my attitude toward John Steinbeck or my sense of his "otherness" until I began the long and deeply involving process of reading his letters. While reading them over a period of years, I found it difficult not to become absorbed into his way of thinking, and every connection between what he had been interested in or worried about and my own thoughts at the same age seemed to draw me further into his identity.

I remember well reading of his thoughts and feelings

during one of the periods in which he was attempting to work as a laborer during the day and then write at night. At about the same age, I too was trying to serve my apprenticeship as a writer by working as a laborer to get enough money to eat and then coming home and trying to write short stories. Working with a pick and shovel was a good antidote for just having received a degree in philosophy, but tough medicine to swallow. After digging for what seemed to me a very long time, my arms and shoulders aching to the point that I could hardly lift another shovelful of dirt, I would become convinced that it was nearly lunchtime, look at my watch, and find to my dismay that it was only 8:30. Even after several months of work I found that my hands were so stiff in the evenings that my fingers couldn't find the typewriter keys or hold a pen. There were times when I could hold it, but I couldn't feel it, so that I either stubbed my pen on the paper or wrote invisibly about an eighth of an inch above the surface.

I found that in similar circumstances Steinbeck had the same frustration and despair. In a letter to a friend he had written that every night he returned to his furnished room "in an aura of the most complete exhaustion imaginable—so much for literary effort." As the weeks went by, he felt both despondency and guilt because he wasn't getting any writing done: "Just now, I want the time or rather the energy to write more than anything on earth."

This and other reflections by the novelist which reflected almost exactly my own state of being at various times in my life began to convince me that I could think as he thought and fill in the gaps of my direct knowledge. I would come to a place in his life where I didn't know what he had done and had no way to find out, and I would ask myself, "What would I do in those circumstances?" When something happened to him, I would ask myself, "How would I have felt about that?"

This way of thinking was of course wrong and terribly destructive to the integrity of my project. But I was convinced for a time not that I was Steinbeck or that his soul had come to visit my mind—the delusion never became that severe—but that I knew so much about him that I could predict his reactions and think as he would think under similar circumstances.

My confidence in my role playing continued for a while until something his widow said brought me up short. It was a small, almost insignificant thing, but it made me see the error of my ways. I had never really thought much about it, but I had always just assumed that John slept in his skivvies. It wasn't something I was going to ask about, since it bordered on an area of privacy that was none of my business, had nothing to do with defining his personality or development as a writer, and was trivial—who cares what he slept in? But the biographer, like the fiction writer or poet, operates with a picture machine in his head. As I read about John, heard stories about him, and then later wrote about him, I always saw the scene, in some detail, in my mind.

So when I heard about something to do with John sleeping or getting out of bed to do something, I had this picture of him in his underwear. After all, *I* slept in my underwear, and it seemed to me to be a masculine and western thing to do. We all know the westerner must be ready to jump up, slip on his boots, defend the homestead, or leap on his horse and ride hell-bent for leather to protect his herd. In my view, only effete easterners wore things like pajamas and nightgowns, then put on velvet robes and slippers every time they got up to go to the bathroom or answer the phone.

One day I was interviewing Elaine Steinbeck about her husband, and she was telling me a story about how he was awakened one night and had to jump out of bed and rush to the door. I said, "Oh my God, there he was, standing in the door with nothing but his jockey shorts on!"

Elaine looked at me for a moment, puzzled, and said, "What in the world do you mean? John always slept in pajamas and when he got up, put on a robe."

"Oh," I said, and explained my picture of him.

She said, "No, you are all wrong. Why, he often wore a robe and didn't get dressed until late morning; sometimes he lounged around in a robe and slippers all day. There were times when he was depressed and didn't feel like it, he wouldn't even get out of bed."

So there I was—I had a picture that was totally false. It was on the scale of mistakes a rather minor one, but it was enough to make me think and question all the assumptions I had been making on the basis of my identification of my life with John's. We were two entirely different people, and I pledged to myself never to forget that. After some thought I realized that my mistaken way of thinking was leading me into a far greater error, that of losing my objectivity. For I was determined to write a book about John Steinbeck, not in praise of him. It was all right to be sympathetic—it would be stupid to spend years and the family fortune to write about someone you didn't care about or despised. But I had to maintain my distance.

5

Biographer as Detective

Since *The Grapes of Wrath* is John's masterpiece, I was naturally interested in finding out as much as possible about how he happened to write it and where and how he got his material. Years ago, when I first read it, I noticed the second part of the novel's dedication, "To Tom, Who Lived It," and it added a little excitement to the novel. I thought, as perhaps most readers also thought, that the dedication referred to some real-life counterpart of the novel's central character, Tom Joad. And in thinking about the novel, I began to consider it, in part, a testimony to a friendship.

Through the years I have had it in my mind's eye that Steinbeck traveled to Oklahoma and hooked up with a family, the Joads, which had been dusted off its farm and was headed west. I saw the writer becoming a companion to the older son, while the family made its way, in an old battered car made into a truck, across the desert and mountains into California. And in my mind's eye I saw John Steinbeck, squatting on his heels with a tin cup in his hand in front of a roadside campfire, probing the heart and mind of a Tom Joad dressed in overalls and looking a lot like Henry Fonda.

But it didn't happen that way. When Carol, John's first wife, corrected me, she destroyed another nice mental picture. Then who was the Tom in the dedication? I asked. Tom Collins, she replied. She went on to tell me that John had gone to the Farm Security Administration in San Francisco to get some information about the Dust Bowl migrants for an article he was writing for the *San Francisco*

News. The FSA people had offered to take him down to the Central Valley to see the situation for himself, assigning one of their management supervisors, Eric Thomsen, to accompany him as his guide. On that trip John had met Tom Collins, manager of one of the government migrant camps, and it was from Collins that John had gotten much of his information for the novel.

That was about all she could tell me, so it was up to me to discover the details of what happened. This effort led me up a side road of research that, off and on, took several years and extended the length of time for the project as a whole. I began by reading everything I could find about the Dust Bowl, about the migration to California, and about government responses to the problem. In my reading I discovered that a key figure in attempts by the state government to deal with the problem was Paul Taylor, professor of economics in the University of California at Berkeley. I found that he was still at the university, an emeritus professor, and I began a correspondence with him that spanned almost a decade.

Taylor had met Collins, although he did not know him well, and was only able to tell me in general terms that Collins had been a camp manager for the Farm Security Administration at several camps in the Central Valley. But he did suggest that I go to the Federal Archives in San Francisco (later moved to San Bruno) and look at the papers from the FSA camp program that might be stored there. I wrote to the archives director about my Steinbeck work and my interest in his connection with Tom Collins and the federal camp program. She wrote back that they had a lot of FSA papers but that it was "pretty perfunctory stuff"—bureaucratic paperwork—and that I was unlikely to find anything of interest in it, but I was welcome to look.

I drove up to San Francisco and found the archives, a warehouse near South City overlooking the old World War II shipyards. After only a few hours of sorting through the stacks of papers, which were brought to me on a large library cart, I realized I had hit the mother lode. I became very excited. Among the papers was a stack of reports from the Arvin Migrant Camp near Bakersfield which Collins had sent in every few weeks. But these were not just dry reports. Collins had included observations of migrant behavior, anecdotes about odd or funny things that had happened in camp, migrant songs and sayings (written in Collins's imitation of Okie dialect). There were also lists of visitors, and, sure enough, for one week in August, 1936, two of the names listed were Eric Thomsen and John Steinbeck. Hot dog!

I was certain no one involved in literary research on Steinbeck had seen or even heard of this material (I learned later that at least one scholar working on California history had used it). I was so exhilarated by my find that I went right in to see the director to tell her about it.

Later I made the connection tighter, when at Carol's suggestion I interviewed Reginald Loftus, a neighbor of the Steinbecks in Los Gatos, and he recalled John coming back from the Central Valley with a pile of carbons of camp reports Collins had given to him. Loftus himself became a camp manager for the FSA, and he was able to give me several leads to other FSA personnel. I went on for the next two years spending much of my time following a chain of leads to various people who had worked with and knew Collins. At the same time I worked out a number of parallels between items in the Collins reports and characters, events, and language in *The Grapes of Wrath*. I also went to the National Archives in Washington, D.C., where I found correspondence with Collins and about him, including evaluations of his work.

On the same trip I stopped by the Library of Congress. I wanted to look at the library's collection of Dorothea Lange's photos. (Her pictures of Dust Bowl landscapes and victims, of migrants in transit and in California, have become classics, as closely connected to the Okies and the suffering of farm laborers as *The Grapes of Wrath*.) One or

Tom Collins with a migrant mother at "Weedpatch," a migrant camp near Arvin, California. Photograph by Dorothea Lange. Courtesy of the Library of Congress, Washington, D.C.

two photos that I had seen had been identified as having been taken in the summer of 1936, and they looked as though they might have been taken at a government camp.

Sure enough, after looking though several hundred photos connected with the subject, I found a series labeled "Arvin Migrant Camp, 1936." Among them—my good luck seemed unbelievable—a half dozen of Tom Collins, alone and working with groups of migrants. Those who thumb through the pictures in my biography, perhaps pausing briefly to look at the one photo of Collins at work that I was able to include, will never know what a miracle it was, at least in my view, to have such a picture at all.

I had discovered that Collins had been a very remarkable man who had not only provided material about the language and everyday behavior of the Okies to Steinbeck, both in his camp reports and in conversation, but also influenced John by his manner of running the camp and by his philosophy. He had a basic Jacksonian sense of democracy which in the camps he translated into camper self-government. He knew that these people had been kicked around by officials and agencies, and so he avoided their deep-seated suspicion of authority by having the migrants adopt their own rules and enforce them themselves.

He also knew that since they had come to California they had been mocked and scorned, and so he was very sensitive to their feelings, demonstrating great tact, even in the face of provocations that would have unsettled or enraged a man with less patience. Although he never became an administrator for the FSA, he had a profound influence on the migrant camp program, since he was used to open and structure new camps as they were built and to train new managers.

John was so impressed by what he had witnessed in August that he returned again in September. On both occasions he not only viewed the government facilities in operation but also was taken to view the nearby squatters' shacks, impromptu camps of weeds, cardboard, and pieces of tin set up usually on the banks of an irrigation ditch, and workers' camps, often almost as squalid, provided by growers on the farms. John began his first draft of *The Grapes of Wrath*, but was interrupted by a trip to Europe, financed by the sale of *Of Mice and Men*, and then by work with George S. Kaufman in New York on the play version of the novel. He returned, with some relief, from the East to join Tom Collins once again for the extended trip through the Central Valley, the one which he led his friends and neighbors to believe he had taken to Oklahoma.

Once I knew the story of John's relationship with Collins, the part played by the camp reports, and the chronology of the various trips to the valley, I felt that I now knew what I had to know to go on with the biography, but I also felt that I had more material than I could include in the book. So I decided to do an article to tell the story of the background of Steinbeck's most important novel, believing that most of what I had discovered was new and that much of it was as important as anything else that I would likely find out about John Steinbeck in relation to his work. I was also concerned to publish my findings as early as possible, because someone else might run across the same material, and I knew that the biography would not be ready for publication for many years. Of all the many things I had discovered about Steinbeck over the previous few years, I thought that this material was probably the most dramatic and important and would provide my best chance for footnote immortality.

I finished my article and along with a series of photos of the Arvin Camp and Collins sent it off to the *Journal of Modern Literature,* where it was accepted for publication almost immediately (I was very concerned to find a periodical that published photographs, which is not very common among literary journals). In the meantime, however, the archivist at the federal facility in San Francisco had apparently been infected with the enthusiasm I had shown in response to my find. About the time my article had gone in for publication, I discovered, not only had she sent out bulletins advertising the existence of the collection to interested parties around the country but actually had sent complete photocopies of the material itself to various libraries and other institutions which had been associated with Steinbeck studies.

Almost immediately, a professor at one of these institutions, having had the material delivered into her lap gratis, took it up and wrote an article of her own (not knowing, of course, of my involvement in the discovery of its relevance to Steinbeck). When I heard of her work, I was panic-stricken—three years and my chance for scholarly immortality were going down the drain. I wrote several times to the editor of the *Journal of Modern Literature* begging him to hurry up and publish. He promised to do the best he could, but he had a big backlog of material, and the publication of the journal was about six months behind schedule. In other words, he really couldn't do anything, was terribly behind in his own work, and probably needed my hysteria as much as he needed a third leg.

It took more than two years for the article to appear (in the spring of 1976)—while my impatience reached mountainous proportions—but it did appear before the competition. In retrospect I can see that none of this has been of the slightest importance to anyone besides myself. Few have read the article, fewer still have seen any significance in it, and no one, so far as I know, has referred to it in print or footnoted it. (My "competitor" graciously acknowledged the existence of my article in hers.) In fact, just the opposite has already occurred. In a recent short biography of Steinbeck the author uses the Tom Collins material and thanks the archivist profusely, giving the impression that he, with her help, discovered it all by himself.

With all that I had discovered about Tom Collins, his relationship with Steinbeck, and his influence on *The Grapes of Wrath*, there were still some blank spaces that nagged at me and wouldn't let me rest. I didn't have the whole story.

In early 1936, Collins seemed to come out of nowhere to become the first migrant camp manager at an FSA camp established near Marysville, at the northern end of the Central Valley. Then, after a successful career of managing sanitary camps all over the state and training new managers, he suddenly left government service in 1941 and seemed to disappear. While I was interviewing camp managers and others who had tried to help the migrants during the period, I found that they almost invariably had known Collins. But try as I might, I couldn't find anyone who knew anything about his background—where he was born, what his schooling was, what kind of job experience he had brought with him. This was very curious because Collins was a very garrulous man. Surely, I thought, he must have said something about his early life to someone.

The mystery of what happened to him after he left the FSA was equally baffling. Several people had heard that Collins had married about the time he left and that he might have purchased a farm near San Juan Bautista, California, south of San Jose. I wrote to all the counties in the area where Collins was last employed (Thornton) and near San Juan Bautista, but I could find no record of his marriage. I wrote again to the counties near San Juan, to Pacific Gas and Electric Company, to various water districts, and to the city of Hollister in an effort to find some record of property ownership, but with no luck.

I wrote back to many of the people I had interviewed earlier about the migrants, Collins, and the camp program, pressing for any scrap of information or hearsay that they might have concerning Collins's fate. Only one piece of information surfaced—a farm labor organizer that I had talked to remembered seeing Collins sometime in the late 1940s at an old hotel in a run-down area of Sacramento where derelicts are often hired by labor contractors to work in the fields. So I wrote to various agencies in Sacramento County, trying to find a record of employment, receipt of county health or welfare services, or death.

I did receive some news this time. A Thomas Collins had applied for a job as a porter with the Sacramento Civil Service in April, 1949, and a Thomas Collins had been treated in a Sacramento hospital in the late 1950s. But the middle initial was different in each case, and by that time I wasn't sure what Collins's middle name was or if he had a middle name. Then, in a roundabout way, I was able to inquire about a possible "rap sheet" on Collins, and although the physical description matched my Collins, I learned little beyond the fact that he had been arrested twice in northern California for traffic offenses.

Then a reporter for the *Sacramento Bee* wrote to me for information. He was writing a feature article on "what had become of the Okies," and I sent him what information I had, at the same time asking whether he knew anything about the fate of Tom Collins. He replied that he had talked to another reporter for the *Bee* who back in the fifties had been working on a story about farm labor. He had run into a wiry, grizzled old-timer, in the same run-down neighborhood mentioned by the labor organizer, who claimed to have been the Tom that Steinbeck wrote about. Perhaps the reporter thought the man meant that he was the model for Tom Joad—he had never heard of Tom Collins. At any rate, the reporter didn't believe him.

At this point the trail grew cold, and I was unable to find out anything further about Collins after he left his manager's job. It seemed as if the last part of his story was sad— perhaps he had ended up a derelict or a migrant like the migrants he had devoted his life to help.

I was unwilling to give up my search entirely, however, and continued my letter writing, now concentrating on federal agencies and records centers, as well as back issues of California newspapers published in towns near where Collins had worked. I was able to get two new pieces of information: one was that he had a doctorate in education from a Teachers' Professional College in Washington, D.C., and the other was that he had been school superintendent for the U.S. naval government on Guam and that a pamphlet published by the Institute for Public Services had described his work in organizing the Guam schools. But an extensive search through various reference works and letters to agencies in Washington, D.C., failed to turn up any information about Teachers' Professional College, which apparently had been long defunct. And although I found out that the State Historical Society of Wisconsin was the official repository for the records and publications of the Institute for Public Services, it had no information regarding the Collins pamphlet.

When it came time to write my article, I really had very little solid information about Tom Collins the man. I had discovered what I thought was a birthplace and birthdate for him, but the records had been destroyed by fire. I talked to Collins's former bosses at the FSA, but they couldn't remember who had hired him or what his qualifications had been. I found that whenever he had been asked by his superiors to furnish biographical information for public relations purposes, he had always responded with a brief summary of his work for the FSA. Furthermore, it seemed to me from the records I could obtain that he had at various times changed his middle name or middle initial, his social security number, his birth date, his place of birth, and the names of his parents.

To add to the confusion, I found that there had been several Tom Collinses around who had roughly matched the description of my Tom Collins, including one who also worked for a short time for the FSA. Then, to throw a little mystery into the confusion, I came across several people who were supposed to have information on Collins but who refused to talk to me about him. Why was it so very difficult to find the basic facts of this man's life? Had he done something so terrible in his early life that he felt he must cover his tracks? I began to consider seriously the possibility that he had been landed on an American beach in 1935 by a Russian or German submarine.

I had exhausted all the leads I had, and I couldn't think of any other direction in which to turn. I had written my article, and I decided to let the investigation drop. I had already spent far too much time on it, and it had been taking me further and further away from my central concern, the life and work of John Steinbeck. Still, I felt dissatisfied.

About this time I was invited to give a talk on Steinbeck at the dedication of the Steinbeck Collection at Stanford University. I had been of some help to the library in acquiring parts of the collection. The invitation had come not from the university itself but from the Associates of the Stanford University Libraries—still, it was an exciting thing for me, an indifferent scholar and obscure student there, to go back to my own university and, after an introduction by Pulitzer Prize winner N. Scott Momaday, to give a speech to a filled auditorium.

It turned out to be exciting in another way also. Unknown to me, there was a reporter in the audience from

Parade Magazine, the supplement put out with many Sunday newspapers throughout the country. My talk had been an abbreviated version of my article on Collins, and suddenly, about a month later, I got a call from an editor at *Parade*, telling me about their article on my speech and asking for a photo of Collins. When it came out, the *Parade* article featured my discovery of the camp manager as the person to whom the second part of the novel's dedication referred, "To Tom, Who Lived It" (actually, that was already known), and his role in providing information to Steinbeck for *The Grapes of Wrath.*

When the article appeared, I was suddenly swept from my determination to ignore anything further on Collins in favor of making progress on my long-neglected biography. The first wave of new information hit me when I got a phone call from Tom Collins's daughter—who, as it turned out, lived two miles from my home. The second wave came with a letter from another daughter, by an earlier marriage, who lived in Pennsylvania. I exchanged several letters with the latter and interviewed the former at some length and had enough information about Collins that I felt I should tack on an "Afterword" to my original article.

I was well into writing my postscript essay when I got another letter. It began, "I am Tom Collins' only daughter." It turned out that the first two daughters had only recently found out about each other and that neither of them had known about the third or she about them. One of the best things to come out of these revelations was that the daughter that lived near me, Patricia Collins Olson, and the last daughter who wrote to me, Mary Alice Johns, discovered each other and became good friends. A pleasant surprise for me was that Mrs. Johns had a cache of written material and memorabilia concerning her father that she offered to me for my use.

Among the things to which I was given access were Steinbeck's letters to Collins, a correspondence I had given up all hope of finding, and the manuscript of an autobiographical novel written by Collins. I found upon reading it

that the manuscript dealt in part with Collins's experiences
with Steinbeck. I had been hoping against hope for years
that somehow I would find someone who could give me an
eyewitness view of Steinbeck in the field with the migrants.
I felt the biography desperately needed that—and here it
was. And there was more. The manuscript had a foreword
by Steinbeck which described his first meeting with Collins
at the Arvin camp. I was ecstatic. I had known about the
foreword from references in letters, but I had assumed that
it, too, had been lost.

I also now knew a good deal about the man Tom Collins,
and what I learned came together as a story more romantic
and implausible than my submarine theory. He had been
in trouble much of his life, although it may have been a
matter more of conscience than of law. The key to the mystery was that Collins was married three times, had three
separate families, and none of the families knew about each
other. Collins had deserted at least one wife and several
children; there was a possible charge of bigamy hanging
over his head; and, needless to say, at various times he
owed money.

It is too bad that at the time he wrote his autobiographical novel Collins felt he still had to hide much of his background (even while using a pen name), for his life was far
more adventurous in fact than as he fictionalized it. The
facts of his birth—place, date, and circumstances—are still
not certain. He may not himself have had that information.
He appears to have been born out of wedlock, in 1895 or
1897, in the vicinity of Baltimore, Maryland, and as an infant was placed by his mother in a Catholic orphanage in
Baltimore. The melodrama of his difficulties at the orphanage is reminiscent of something out of Charles Dickens.

He went from the orphanage to a boarding school, Mount
Saint Joseph College, in Baltimore, and from there to Saint
Charles Seminary, in Maryland, to be trained for the priesthood. After two years or so, however, he gave up the
priesthood to go to college and become a teacher. All we
know about his college education is that he possessed a

doctoral diploma from Teachers' Professional College, in Washington, D.C. Since the college is no longer in existence, it has been impossible to find out how valid this degree was; however, since the name does not appear in any of the appropriate reference works for those years, there would seem to be a possibility that it was a diploma mill. Whatever its worth, Collins used the degree repeatedly to obtain various jobs throughout his lifetime.

He met his first wife, Edith M. Bentzel, while he was a patient in the Victor Cullen Tuberculosis Sanitarium, in Sabillasville, Maryland. After his condition was arrested, he remained at the sanitarium to work in the combined post office and pharmacy. He was married to Edith early in 1915, and they had two daughters, Naomi and Anna. During this period he became a schoolteacher and taught two years at Wolfsville Elementary School, in Maryland, and then at the Winchester Military Academy.

He abandoned his family shortly after the birth of his second daughter and eloped with Nancy Duvall Means, sixteen, the daughter of a prominent social-register family in Maryland. The story is that they met in a railroad station, Collins running from his family and Miss Means running from a chaperone who was escorting her home on vacation from an exclusive girls' school. They ran off together to San Juan, Puerto Rico, where they were married by the bishop of San Juan. The couple was being chased by private detectives hired by the bride's father, and so they fled from Puerto Rico to Caracas, Venezuela, where they hid in a slum while Collins worked in a nearby oil field.

After several months in Caracas, the couple had to move on again, traveling across South America under very difficult conditions, including a journey through the Amazon rain forest. Then Collins and his young wife came back to the United States, hiding in backwater towns in the Southwest and California. At this point Collins applied for a job overseas with the U.S. Navy school system and went first to Nome, Alaska, and later to Guam, where he was superintendent of schools for several years. While they were living on Guam, Collins and his wife spent as much time as possible traveling, going to Australia, New Zealand, Hong Kong, and the Philippines.

Returning to the United States from Guam in 1929, Collins started a school for delinquent boys of wealthy parents, the Oaks School for Boys, in Spring Valley, California, just outside San Diego. After only two or three years of operation, the school went bankrupt, leaving Collins deep in debt. At the same time, his wife's parents had finally caught up with their daughter and were attempting to talk her into leaving her husband. Under pressure of bankruptcy and the strife caused by the interference of his wealthy in-laws, as well as a serious drinking problem, Collins once again left his family and was subsequently divorced by Nancy. They had had two children while they were on Guam, Patricia and another daughter, who died in infancy.

Collins found a job as head of the Federal Transient Service Facility in San Diego and a few months later became manager of the facility in Los Angeles. (These facilities were the soup kitchens set up during the early years of the Depression to feed the hungry.) Following this work, he joined the Resettlement Administration in 1935 (the name was changed shortly thereafter to the Farm Security Administration) and worked for this agency, as I have indicated, as a camp manager until he left in 1941. In 1939 he met a public health nurse, Lena Ann Pimentel, and they were married January 10, 1940, in Yuma, Arizona (no wonder I couldn't find a record of the marriage anywhere in California). A daughter, Mary Alice, was born November 26, 1940.

When he left the FSA, he and his wife moved to a fifteen-acre apricot ranch owned by his wife (no wonder I couldn't find any record of property ownership in his name) near San Juan Bautista, and he retired to a life of maintaining the farm and writing. However, in 1943, perhaps because of a lack of success in writing and farming, Collins moved his family. to the area near Fresno. There he was employed first as a consultant to California Cotton and then to the California Wine Institute. In July, 1946, he was divorced from his third wife and spent the following ten years managing hotels throughout California—in Salinas, Marysville, Willows, and Sacramento. In 1958 he had surgery for cancer at French Hospital, in San Francisco, and again in 1959 in Sacramento. He died of cancer September 14, 1961, in Sacramento.

Mary Alice Johns, the daughter of Collins's third marriage, wrote to me of her father:

> He was always so thin, just a bit of a man, never weighed over 140 pounds. . . . most of his life was spent in the area of 125. All of the pictures I have show him as needing suspenders to hold his pants up. I never remember my Daddy having anything but a lovely thick head of white hair.

> Over the years, the people I have met that Daddy worked with, the neighbors who knew him, and my family, have always had kind things to say about him. He was kind, gentle, witty (could tell stories by the hour), compassionate, loving, always concerned about their welfare. . . . There is a derogatory word about my Daddy (but only one)—he drank.

The mixture of elements one finds in reading Collins's autobiographical novel—the romance, the self-dramatization, the folk realism, and the political utopianism—seems to sum up Collins's life, his achievements and his failures. He was a dreamer, a talker, and a drinker. He had a genius for getting along with and helping people who were down and out but was a failure, for the most part, in managing the relations of his own personal life. He was part educator, part artist, and part confidence man. He was ragged Tom the orphan boy, who survived the discipline of Catholic institutions and a hard childhood to achieve respectability as husband, father, and teacher, only to break away from his conventional life into the adventure of dime novels—eloping with a young heiress, running from detectives, and escaping by way of a South American rain forest.

Although I saw enough documentation and heard enough testimony to convince me that the broad outline, at least, of

Collins's story as I have presented it is true, nevertheless, the story of his life has an astonishing literary quality. On the one hand there are the vivid colors of *True Romance*, *Real Detective*, and *Jungle Stories*; on the other, the more somber tones of Don Passos, Dreiser, and Fitzgerald. There is something almost archetypal in Collins's itinerancy, his reaching out for the dream, first for himself and then for others, and his final submersion.

While in the Fitzgerald novel *The Great Gatsby* James Gatz invents a new and more glamorous self as Jay Gatsby, Tom Collins becomes Windsor Drake, that aristocratically named hero who, in the Collins novel, rises from the persecutions heaped upon an abandoned child to become a famous social reformer. The major difference, of course, was that Collins's dream evolved into something a good deal more unselfish than Gatsby's, and while he failed some people, he directly and indirectly helped a great many more.

6

Gwyn and Kate: Two Women in His Life

For a long time I put off trying to get in touch with John's second wife, Gwyndolyn, because, in addition to my usual dread of interviewing, I thought she might very well be hostile. I didn't want her to turn me down, but I didn't want to interview her either if she was going to bring me into the bitterness that I knew she had for other members of the family.

Most everyone I had talked to about John, both friend and relative, had expressed the opinion that his second marriage had been a mistake. Most everyone seemed to like Carol, although many thought she was hard to take at times, but Gwyn seemed to be on nearly everyone's blacklist. John's two older sisters obviously disapproved of her, although it was part of their code of family, covering even former wives, not to say too much against her. Elizabeth seemed to suggest that Gwyn had more or less seduced her brother from his marriage with Carol (which I later found not to be true) and that her influence on him had been destructive. More she wouldn't say.

Others I interviewed suggested, in hushed tones and with the provision that I not quote them, that Gwyn had been the model for the monster Cathy in *East of Eden*, a suggestion that shocked me when I first heard it—how much he must have hated her! But I had also learned through letters and his close friends how much she had gone out of her way to hurt him and make his life, every day and in every way possible, miserable. I really was in no hurry to face the monster, as she had been described, in her cave, and so I procrastinated, having some justification for my delay in that I didn't have a phone number or address for her or any easy means of acquiring them.

I was discovering that there was a great split, with those who were related to Gwyn, who had known Gwyn before her marriage, and who got to know John while he was married to Gwyn on the one side (with a few exceptions) and those who were part of John's own family, who knew him most of his life, and who had come to know him while he was married to Elaine on the other. By and large, people on the one side did not communicate with those on the other. I had not yet reached across the division, although I knew that I would have to, sometime.

The problem of leaping across the family gap and of getting in touch with Gwyn was solved for me. A letter from Gwyn came to me at the university. In formal, legalistic language (typed on an electric typewriter by a secretary), the letter warned me of dire consequences if I did not make sure that everything I wrote about her met with her approval. She ended by reminding me that she held all the copyrights for unpublished and published material by her husband from the time they met in 1938 through 1965.

As I discovered later, the letter was rather typical of Gwyn in several ways. She had a litigious streak in her which had been reinforced by her success in court against her husband, and she could be a bully if she thought she had the upper hand. By having custody of their two children, she had been able to exercise a good deal of power over her former husband for many years, and by never remarrying, she had forced him to pay a substantial alimony until the day he died. In dealing with me, however, she had used a bluff—I knew she did not have copyright control. Actually, she could have just written and invited me to come and talk to her, and I would have obliged. But that wasn't her style.

Rather than taking offense at her approach, I decided to turn the other cheek and wrote to her in conciliatory terms, telling her that I had been trying to get her address (which was true) and that I wanted very much to interview her (only partly true—I also had dreaded it). She wrote back inviting me to come to Palm Springs, where she was living, and we made final arrangements over the phone.

I had never been to Palm Springs before, and so with my usual overconscientiousness I arrived about an hour and a half early. Since my appointment was at 9:30 A.M., this had meant leaving San Diego about 4:00. I went first to find the house, a white neo-adobe in a modest neighborhood, and then went back to the main street to have breakfast in a coffee shop. What I observed seemed to fit the caricature of Palm Springs that most everyone in southern California is familiar with. The major streets near the center of town were clogged with Cadillacs and Mercedeses, all going about five miles per hour. When I got out of my car to go eat, I saw only two kinds of people—those in their fifties and sixties with deep tans and lots of jewelry and very confident-looking high school kids in shorts and alligator T-shirts. I wondered what had happened to the generations between?

I paid my bill, which was almost as high as it would have been in New York, and drove back to the house. The Mexican-American housekeeper answered the door and showed me into the living room, which was bright and cheerful. I had seen photos of Gwyn as she was when John married her. She had been pretty—regular features, light-brown hair, and, except for rather thick ankles, an almost perfect figure. The woman who now came in from her bedroom to greet me was short and very heavy. She wore a muumuu, a shapeless print dress that came almost to the ground, and the most striking feature of her almost colorless face was the rose-tinted frames of her glasses. Her hair had been bleached to a light blonde and surrounded her face in loose curls.

She made me feel welcome and was very gracious. I certainly didn't need to worry about getting her to talk. We started in at a little after 9:30 A.M., and she talked almost continuously, with little prompting and almost no questions

from me, until almost 10:00 that night. It was as if someone
had pulled the plug on a dam, and a torrent poured out,
and on and on. It was clear that she wanted desperately to
bring her point of view to me—she knew very well what
the others had told me, and this, for the former actress, was
a kind of command performance.

She did very well. Normally after a couple of hours, I
would have gotten restless, but she was very entertaining.
She had been taping her memoirs, and so everything was
fresh in her mind, and she moved from time to time, incident to incident, almost without thought, effortlessly. She
made me like her—I really couldn't help myself. She was
an accomplished storyteller, and I think I laughed harder
that day than I ever did before or ever have since. After it
was all over, I thought I could see why John had fallen for
her. As attractive as she might have been, I don't think it
was her looks so much as that she was just someone who
could be a lot of fun to be with. And despite the hardness
that had set in over the years, there was just a touch of
little-girl vulnerability that might lead a man to think,
probably mistakenly, that here was someone that needed
protecting.

But it was her joie de vivre that was catching and made
nearly everything she talked about, no matter how foolish,
funny and enjoyable. She was proud of having drawn her
husband out of himself, out of his moodiness and shyness,
by pushing him to go out. She recalled in some detail the
parties they had gone to in New York. Many of the guests
were writers or show-business people, and they would take
turns performing, often finding props and costumes in the
furnishings of the host's apartment. One particular evening
she had come to the party with a marten stole:

> I went into the dining room, found a compote of fruit which I
> turned upside down on my head, put the marten on, and grabbed
> a fork out of the fireplace. Marc [Connelly] found a bathmat,
> which he turned this way [to serve as armor], and he got a cook-
> ing pot, and we came out and did the Valkyrie. . . . It was all

John and Gwyn in Hollywood before their marriage, ca. 1940. Courtesy of Sandy Oliver.

double-talk—we all knew the music. . . . And all the crazy things
that Abe Burrows would do—you know, his crazy songs: "Walk-
ing Down Memory Lane Without a God Damned Thing on My
Mind." And the things he did with Dorothy Parker: "If I Had to
Do It All Over Again, I'd Do It All Over You." And "The Gypsy
Fiddle Cried" and "Hans the Huntsman."

   Everybody got up, and who the hell needed a nightclub! We
were an act in ourselves. Now John would seldom participate.
Occasionally, he had two little things he did. He would talk about
some of the men—the trappers he knew when he was young—
their hallucinations after drinking canned heat and that kind of
stuff, and then he had his inevitable "The Seagull over the Monterey Picnic." But his *enjoyment* was divine, and he loved that
more than anything in the world, and I'm not putting, you know,
four-leaf clovers on my shoulders, but I *made* him do this, and
that's when people loved him most.

   Gwyn also talked about the practical joking that went on,
particularly during those times when they were living temporarily with the Frank Loessers in Hollywood or living
next door to the Nathaniel Benchleys in New York. There
was often a kind of undeclared warfare between the men
and the women. On one occasion, for example, Gwyn had
brought young Thom, about a year and a half old, out to the
West Coast to let John's sister see him, and she ended up at
the Loessers', where John came to join them. About the
second day, John and Frank went out to have a few drinks
in the late afternoon, promising to return and take their
wives out to dinner. But they came home late, "feeling no
pain," and by that time Gwyn and Lynn had already eaten
with the children. The women received their husbands
very coldly, expecting an apology, but when Frank and
John found that their wives wouldn't have anything to do
with them, they simply turned around and went out to dinner by themselves.

   The wives were furious and tried to figure out how to get
even. John and Frank were sleeping in separate beds in the
same room, so their wives short-sheeted their beds. They

decided that that was not nearly enough. They boiled up all
the spaghetti they could find and put it in the men's beds.
By this time, the two nurses in charge of the children were
beginning to join in the fun, and they helped Gwyn and
Lynn gather all of the husbands' clothes out of the dresser
drawers, soak them in water, and put them back in the
drawers. "We were like boarding school girls with those
two old nurses. We put limburger cheese in their bedroom
slippers." Then they gathered all the food and liquor and
locked themselves in Lynn's bedroom:

Off of her bedroom was an outside stairs which led up into what
Lynn had made into a sewing room . . . so we thought, nothing is.
going to happen from the inside; they are going to come get us
from the outside. So Lynn gets up and busily puts all the locks on
the doors. We hear the car drive up, and we pour ourselves a
very stiff drink, and we wait for a pounding on the door. Nothing
happened. Absolute quiet. 2 o'clock, 3 o'clock is ticking—meantime, nothing, but *nothing*.

Next morning we come down for breakfast looking radiant, and
eventually Frank appears—John, of course, appeared first.
"Good morning, ladies." Nothing, but *nothing*. I looked at Lynn
and she looked at me, and we can't wait to get to the two nurses
who had been up since six. Any reaction? Anything? Nothing—
not a stir. Two days go by without any comment. That evening was
one when John met Humphrey Bogart and Lauren Bacall, and we
all have dinner together at Mike Romanoff's. Nothing is said.
Nothing. They hadn't even called for the maid to change their
beds. We had boiled five pounds of spaghetti—that's a lot of
spaghetti!

The third day the two women decided it was safe to leave
the house, asking the nurses to keep an eye out for any
strange activity. That night there was to be a big opening at
the Los Angeles Philharmonic, and before they left, Frank
reminded them that they had to get home in time to change
into formal dress and that they were having people over for
cocktails at 5:30. John added, "We want you girls looking
gorgeous tonight!" Later, the wives came home from shop-

ping, and Gwyn went upstairs to change in the sewing room, where her clothes were, and Lynn began to change in her dressing room. Suddenly, Gwyn heard a loud, "Ha, Ha, Ha!" from Lynn in the bathroom—all the towels had been sewed together. "I went into the closet," Gwyn recalled,

and Lynn said, "Look what's happened." You know those guys had spent four hours, and there wasn't anything that we owned, and I mean of the most intimate, that wasn't sewn together. I went to pick up my shoes and twenty-four pairs came out! I went to get one brassiere out of the drawer and a dozen came out right after me. They had spent the whole afternoon. Everything we had had been sewn together—hats, bags, gloves. Our evening clothes— we couldn't get into our evening dresses. You went to put your foot in, and they were sewn together. The next day we went through the closet. Lynn, who had a beautiful body, used to wear gorgeous belts. Two weeks later she was still unstitching the belts. How those two sons of bitches did this in the length of time we were gone, I'll never know—with needle and thread! And the nurses never knew a thing about it.

Although such stories were entertaining, I felt after a time that I should press her more toward talking about her husband as writer—where he got his ideas for particular works, his work habits. We talked about his writing letters in the morning to warm up, and about various tricks he used at times to procrastinate. He used fountain pens during this period, and Gwyn remembered him sighing and saying that there was "just so long that you can fill up a pen." Then he would laugh and say, "But how many times?"

I asked her if he ever became impatient or moody when he was working on something. "He couldn't stand houseguests," she replied:

I think he was possibly one of the finest disciplinarians as far as self-work was concerned—well, to the sacrifice of us all, I might add. He could raise hell. There is no doubt about it, but when he came through after a day's work, he was literally exhausted. He didn't *want* to talk. Every bit of his energy had gone into that pen and come out the back of his brain. . . . He didn't like people popping in on him; he *never* did. He just didn't want to talk. He either wanted to be alone with me, or we would go out to dinner—he would just sort of stare into space.

Then she told me that among their other problems they had the problem that she was a "night person" and he liked to get up early and wanted her up, too. "I was used to sleeping until eleven o'clock," she recalled,

and he was up on his toes at six. His greatest energy was then. And then he had his coffee and maybe a hot bath. Maybe he wouldn't even get dressed. Maybe he wouldn't shave, if he felt it was going good. And [later] he would buzz me or come in and get me up, and we'd talk for an hour, maybe. About a lot of things— about what he is going to do, or a scene he wanted to get in.

Of course, she added, "he always had to have his nest someplace where you couldn't get in and clean it except once a week, and the coffee pot was forever going and always ranch coffee."

"Ranch coffee?" I asked.

"Boiled coffee with the egg in it," she explained. Sometimes "he would drink it straight with condensed milk and brown sugar . . . he wasn't about to sit down to three fried eggs and a half pound of bacon. At that hour of the morning he wasn't ready for it. Sometimes he'd take a break, or he'd holler out, 'Honey, it's going good, uh—don't wait lunch,' or something like that, and he'd come out and he'd be limp."

As enjoyble as much of it was, the day was not without its ominous and painful aspects. About an hour after I arrived, she began drinking a sip of vodka about every ten minutes. She offered me a drink on several occasions, but I declined. What I really wanted, starting about noon, was something to eat, but she never offered. Finally, at nine that evening, out of desperation, I offered to take her out to dinner, but she replied that she never went out to eat because she had a special diet. Yes, she did. And so we went on for an hour more, until I finally excused myself and made an appointment for a follow-up interview the next day.

Since it was a Saturday night, I should have known

enough to arrange for a motel room that morning when I arrived. I drove up and down, back and forth through and around town, but I could not find a single place that had a vacancy. At last, I had to take off down the highway and drove almost an hour until I found a place out in the desert that had a room. By that time, I had been up for almost twenty hours and was so exhausted that I flopped into bed without eating.

After my initial interviews with Gwyn, I always intended to go back and see her again but could never quite get up the courage. But we did correspond a bit and talk on the phone. Unfortunately, not all of our phone conversations were happy ones. If I called her (always after noon—I came to realize that she had made a great sacrifice in getting up so early on the first day that I had interviewed her) or she called me in the daytime, it worked out all right. But she got in the habit of calling me every month or so at three in the morning. She seemed to be in a daze, almost incoherent, with heavy breathing and long pauses between mumbled words.

When a phone rings at three in the morning, your first thought is of doom. Something terrible has happened to someone dear to you, and that realization sinks to the bottom of your stomach. At first it is a shock. Then it becomes uncomfortable. For the first few times, I sat on a stool near the one phone in our house, which was in the kitchen, shivering (naturally, all I had on was my jockey shorts), and patiently tried to talk and make sense of the gibberish that was coming over the phone. This would go on for a half hour or more, until I would finally just break off the conversation and hang up. My tolerance time got less and less, and after about a year, the phone calls stopped. My wife was pleased.

For the most part I had proceeded chronologically in my study of Steinbeck, or tried to. But occasionally something would surface which would take me ahead of myself or back to an earlier period. Such was the case when Stanford

Library acquired the correspondence between John and Katherine Beswick, which took me back to John's college days and the long period of apprenticeship which followed.

Both John and Katherine had been members of the Stanford English Club, an organization of students and faculty members interested in literature and creative writing, and it was probably at the meetings of the club that the two met. Although they dated, their relationship was not, for its time, a typical college romance. By the time John met her, Kate—as he called her—had become skeptical of males and soured on romance, partly through experience and partly through the bitter counsel of a young Stanford English professor, Margery Bailey, who had one unhappy love affair after another.

After a wary beginning, John and Kate established a friendship and sexual relationship between independent equals and were determinedly modern in their avoidance of the courtship ritual. Nevertheless, it was with a certain amount of male pride that John claimed later in a letter to Kate that he had provided a timely and successful antidote to Margery Bailey's poison—that sex was a degrading and thoroughly disgusting activity. Not only were they lovers, but they were interested in each other's writing. John read and discussed at length his short stories with her, and Kate, for her part, was a poet whose work he genuinely admired.

I was able to find out little about Katherine beyond what was revealed in the exchange of letters and in her manuscripts, which were also purchased by the library. The yearbook provides the information that she graduated with a degree in French in 1923, that she was a member of Cap and Gown honorary society, and that she had written the class will. The university registrar was able to add only that, when she enrolled, her family was living in Tustin, California, a small town in Orange County surrounded by citrus groves. Her letters to John reveal that she was estranged from her parents, although they provided a small allowance for her while she served her writing apprenticeship in New York following graduation. One can only

Katherine Beswick. Sanford University yearbook photograph, ca. 1924. Courtesy of Stanford University Archives, Stanford, California.

John at his typewriter in his room at Stanford, ca. 1923. Courtesy of Glenn Graves.

read between the lines of her references to her parents and guess that she may have been too liberated and liberal for her parents' tastes.

The affair between John and Kate appears to have lasted only a few months during one of John's periodic one- or two-quarter-long enrollments at the university, and in the summer of 1924 he went back to work in the sugar beet fields in the Salinas Valley, leaving Kate, who was working temporarily as an assistant to the dean of women, undecided what to do or where to go next. They did not keep in touch after Kate went on to New York and John returned for what was to be his final quarter at Stanford, leaving without a degree in 1925. The following summer he worked as a handyman at Fallen Leaf Lodge, near Lake Tahoe, and then in the fall, he too went to New York to seek his fortune as a writer.

It would make a fine story if the two resumed their relationship in New York, but although John had heard that Kate was somewhere in the city, he was unable to find her.

He had no further contact with her until after he had returned to California and was working as a caretaker on an estate on the shore of Lake Tahoe. He had finished his first novel, *Cup of Gold,* and had written to a friend in New York, Amasa ("Ted") Miller, asking him if he would act informally as his agent. Miller gave Kate news of John, and she wrote to him offering to type a finished copy of his manuscript.

She not only cared for John as a person—not always an easy task during his college years, when he tended to posture as an iconoclast and campus bohemian—but had become devoted to her vision of his potential as a writer. This, then, was the measure of her devotion: to take on, gratis, the extended labor of typing a long manuscript, and type it from John's almost illegible handwriting.

With her offer and his grateful acceptance, they began a correspondence that lasted four years. Several times they discussed the possibility of John's returning to New York, and he tried to talk her into coming back to California. But he recalled his ordeal in the city with horror—it had been a nightmare of long hours of physical labor and, quitting that, near starvation—and she had had a falling out with her parents and was reluctant to come near them again.

Katherine typed his manuscript and, as the correspondence indicates, did some editorial work on it as well. So taken was she with him personally that she proposed that he should be the father of her children. So taken was she with the talent she detected in his writing that she offered to quit her own writing and go to work to support him, at long distance if need be. To her proposals he replied:

No, I do not see how we can arrange your support of me. . . . If it were money, I should take it, because one can make more money, but I will not let you gamble with your art which seems to me a finer art than mine. There is no question of masculine posturing here. . . . I am delighted to have been chosen as the father of your children, or child, as the case may be.

Katherine's art did have some merit. During her time in New York, which was about eight years, she produced sixty-four poems, twenty-two short stories, and three essays. Mention in her letters of sales of poems suggests that at least some of her work was published, although not enough, apparently, to give her hope of eventual success. She was one of those many—hundreds, perhaps thousands, in each generation—with some writing talent but not quite enough, who for years persevere in the face of poverty, lack of recognition, and discouragement, but who eventually must drop away, never having made the mark on literature that they worked so hard to achieve.

Yet one must admire her. It took considerable courage to go to New York alone. She was independent-minded and something of a feminist who had felt the sting of the masculine world, as she makes clear in one of her early poems:

The Same Old Song

Curly-locks, darling,
If you will be mine,
You shall write pretty words
On a lace valentine.

You shall write little sonnets
And sign them in pink,
To keep your white fingers
From masculine ink.

I shall cherish your talents,
But let me make clear
That the writing of books is
A man's work, my dear.

Much of her poetry treats the subjects of men and romance with a bittersweet irony and wit that is reminiscent of Dorothy Parker. But there are other poems, closer to A. E. Housman, that depart from light verse to enter a darker realm:

Beggars' Horses

Night is too full of wishing; I have lain
Long hours and heard the gallop, through the dark,

Of fleshless horses that escape the rein,
And running after them a ragged, stark
And cheerless throng of beggars crying loud
To halt the phantom horses in their flight.
Weary, but surging on, the beggar crowd
Pursues the fleeter horses through the night.

And near and very far, my restless heart
Hears the great clamor of the unfulfilled,
And far away and near I feel the smart
Of hard drawn breath in runners little skilled.
All through the night the cries go up outside
Of beggars for the horses they would ride.

Such a poem reminds us that to live as a stranger in New
York in the mid-1920s with very little money and only the
slim hope of some success as a poet could be a gloomy, cold,
and lonely experience. Katherine writes John every now
and again of an editor's interest in her work—he will take her
out or meet her over lunch to discuss her poetry (one reads
between the lines and has a vision of a literary gentleman,
twirling his mustache, more interested in the poet than the
poetry). But nothing came of such opportunities.

It is little wonder, under the circumstances, that her
brightest poems are those that look back to childhood. One
of three series of poems among her manuscripts is that col-
lected under the title "The Book of Joanna Medora Mc-
Dee," and it is in these verses, written from the point of
view of a child facing the adult world, that Katherine seems
to display the greatest talent:

A Word Called Chair

A chair could be any old sort of a thing—
A cave in the hill; a throne for a king;
A ship, or a train, or a castle wall,
Or a circus tent, or a water-fall. . . .

And wouldn't you think, with the names to choose,
They'd have found some meaning-er word to use

> For the millions of things that are really there
> Than a plain little ugly word called "chair"?

After Kate typed John's manuscript, Ted Miller took it over and tried to place it with a publisher. In the meantime, John, weary of being so much alone, left his caretaking to take a job with the state fish and game department at the Tahoe City fish hatchery, where there would be some year-round company. During the summer the hatchery was something of a tourist attraction, and John met and fell in love with one of the visitors, a young woman, Carol Henning, who would become his first wife.

He had not written to Kate for some time when he finally broke his silence to tell her that he was in love. There was something very touching about the relationship that had developed between these two young people, separated by thousands of miles, as they supported one another in the terrible struggle to become artists. Their letters, from the wilds of the Sierra to Greenwich Village, seem to flash warm messages of understanding from one dark planet across endless space to another dark planet.

To his news, Kate replied:

My dear:

Your news letter of the 26th has just come, and I am so awfully relieved to know that nothing more catastrophic than a love affair is responsible for your silence. And why, dear, should I hold it against you that you are "so damned Irish"? It is, rather, that you're so delightfully Irish. I should be infinitely disappointed in you, I think, if you failed to go on, from one love affair into the next, so long as the power is on you. It's one of those things which just must be, and which is wholly delightful and desirable. . . .

And you must have gathered that my love for you is of a somewhat peculiar brand. It would be battered and broken by double-dealing and disloyalty—but otherwise it is singularly undemanding.

Why should you have thought yourself too old to be stricken? It is not only women who "go on forever." The damned, delightful Irish male has a very similar tendency. But it is true, as you say, that one does find old age an impediment to haste. I am thrilled that you can cast it aside for a long enough time to be in love. I am afraid I can never again be capable of a violent and romantic love affair—and it is very sad. I have a disturbing tendency to look at myself and laugh—and that rather wet-blankets the more romantic aspects of an affair. . . .

Naturally I shall write, as well as I can—although, as you know, a wholly one-sided correspondence tends to lose its eclat to some extent. Still, I am a very capable person, and I shall do what I can.

However, when you are a bit calmer, I do wish you would tell me about everything—the lady herself, for instance, and the progress of the affair. . . . Personally, of course, I am a little opposed to your marrying although, as I have prophesied, I think it inevitable within the next few years. It has a tendency to spoil things a bit; one can never be quite so free with a married man. However, I leave the matter entirely in your hands. . . .

I woke up this morning with my miraculous burst of energy somewhat diminished—which is just as well. It had a tendency to make me too restless. I shall get more writing done, I think, now that I am not consumed with a desire to be going places and doing things. I am unendingly grateful to you and Henry Morgan [the central character in John's *Cup of Gold*] for bringing me once more to the consciousness that I really can do something. I am convinced, now, as I used to be years ago, that I shall do something good eventually. Life is a very sound investment—in other words, I am happy.

Always I love you, dear

Katherine

John decided that if he was going to make any progress at all with Carol he would have to leave the mountains, go to San Francisco, and try to find a job. On September 1, 1928, he wrote to Kate:

I'm going tomorrow. I'm terrified at my impending poverty. Such things as clothes— I haven't any of them. But why go on.

I'll buy a pair of corduroys and pretend to be a college boy. But the girl, I rather hate to embarrass her. I'm really very fond of her. I intend to live with her, and the trouble is that she makes three times as much money as I can hope to. . . . Anyway she's a nice girl and doesn't mind my poverty in the least.

The new opus is going to begin just about as quickly as I can find a typewriter table.

Through the help of his brother-in-law, he was able to find a job in the city working as a warehouseman for the Bemis Bag Company, lifting and moving heavy bales of jute. But as in New York, where he had also worked as a laborer for a time, he found that long days of hard physical work and evenings of writing didn't mix well. The longer he found himself in a condition where he was too tired to write, the more despondent he became. He reported his situation to Kate:

For eight hours every day I push about trucks on which are bales of jute which weigh about eighteen hundred pounds. I have been at it only a week, and gradually I seem to be getting slightly used to it. But for this week anyway, I have come home in an aura of the most complete exhaustion imaginable. So much for literary effort. It just ain't possible yet.

A couple of weeks later he wrote: "I fully intended to go to the library, but the tiredness was too great. . . . San Francisco is very lovely now. I wish I could see some of it. But I work in a basement and it is nearly dark when I get home." And at the end of September: "Am almost convinced that one cannot do eight hours of heavy labor and write, too. There isn't enough energy to go around. . . . Just now, I want the time or rather the energy to write more than anything on earth."

Then he wrote Kate in mid-October:

I don't know. I am approaching thirty. I shall be twenty-seven in February. Not the desire but the consciousness of an ability to write is slowly dying out of me. It is being pushed out by simple fatigue. I am making one last try to get words on paper, this try to last until Christmas, and if it prove as futile as the attempts of the last two months, I am resolved to follow my own advice. It would not be a bad thing.

There is nothing in the other letters which have survived that would indicate what advice to Kate he is referring to here, but he was clearly at the end of his rope, and whatever course of action he was considering, it would appear to have been something drastic. From the time he was fifteen, he had been determined to become a writer, and he had become so totally inspired by that goal that no other direction in life would seem to have even occurred to him. Now he found it physically impossible to go on.

Kate, anxious about his despair, had first offered to support him somehow and then, when he turned her down, had sent him money. In mid-December, still unable to write, he decided to quit his job, move into his parents' beach house in Pacific Grove, and write until the money ran out. He wrote to Kate:

Your letter came tonight. I am sitting in the lobby of the Trinidad Hotel on Broadway, doing my corresponding. You see I have a fire place at home, but nothing to put in it. And the nights are very bitter. . . .

This is Monday—on Saturday I shall go home for Christmas. And immediately afterward I shall go to P. G. and start writing. I have $30 left of the $50 you sent. Perhaps I can stretch it over a month. Perhaps—I arrived at this decision last Friday. I haven't the least idea what I shall do when the 30 runs out for there are no jobs in P. G. But the moment I had decided, everything changed, and since then I have hardly been able to keep from throwing the bales through the roof. I shall write and write and write.

The money from Kate, which she could hardly have afforded to send, came at a crucial time and probably saved him from complete despair. After her gift of money ran out, John's father, impressed by his son's intense devotion to his art and by the boost in morale that Kate's gift had provided, decided to give John twenty-five dollars a month to live on, as an "advance against future royalties." This continued even after John's marriage until he and Carol were able to support themselves with odd jobs, living for the most part on the edge of disaster until his first success, at the age of thirty-three, with *Tortilla Flat.*

Not long after John's marriage in 1930, Kate gave up her writing and moved to Minneapolis, and once again the two lost track of each other. From the time that they had parted when John left Stanford for the summer in 1924, they were never to see each other again. We know, of course, that John went on, after *Tortilla Flat,* to the great period of his career, publishing *In Dubious Battle, Of Mice and Men* (winning the Drama Critics' Circle Award in 1937 for the play version), *The Long Valley* (which included the first book publication of *The Red Pony*), and his masterpiece, *The Grapes of Wrath* (winning the Pulitzer Prize). He became in his later years one of the two or three best-known American authors throughout the world and was awarded, in 1962, the Nobel Prize for Literature. It may be that, in the achievement of all of this, Kate's contribution had made a difference.

As for what happened to Kate, I was able to find out very little. After Minneapolis, she lived for a time in Redwood City, near Stanford, on the San Francisco peninsula, and died sometime in the mid-1970s, several years after John's death in 1968. At the time of her death, she was living in Hawaii and apparently had never married.

When she was young, she had written:

> The world grows old in ashen gray,
> I shall go down another way.
> I'll give to age a scarlet name
> And wear a dress of singing flame.

We don't know what her last years were like, but we can hope that her spirit remained indomitable and independent to the end.

7

Coping With the Famous

As I progressed in my interviews to the middle and later periods of Steinbeck's life, I found myself more and more involved with people who were in the public eye. I have never been a celebrity seeker. In fact, if I were in a restaurant and someone told me that so-and-so was in the next room, I am sure I wouldn't take the trouble to get up and look. So at first my attitude was more of annoyance than pleasure or even curiosity, when I had to try to arrange such interviews.

I knew from my friend and colleague Richard Astro, who was also doing a book on Steinbeck, that a lot of work can be involved in getting to the famous and that, once you get there, the results can be disappointing. They are often weary of being interviewed and wary of being misquoted, and so unlikely to approach such sessions with any degree of enthusiasm. Then, from the angle of the interviewer, the famous do often have an aura about them which is intimidating, and this, added to my regular interviewing jitters, made the whole prospect unappealing.

But the main problem, of course, is getting to see them in the first place. The barriers set up were such that if I hadn't had help from Mrs. Steinbeck, or if one famous person hadn't called up or made arrangements for me with another, I wouldn't have had a chance. Not only are there unlisted numbers (which are often changed with regularity), but there are tiers of secretaries, associates, assistants, agents, and managers. Even an unlisted number will get you only an answering service. You don't call the famous; they call you back—sometimes.

If you do get a call back, nine times out of ten it will be a secretary who doesn't know where his or her boss is or when he or she can call you. And the secretary's boss is not the person you are after, only an associate or assistant. But you can leave a message. And then wait. If you get another call, again the chances are that this time it is a personal secretary or the assistant who does know where the boss is but is unwilling to admit to anything or arrange anything definite.

After a time you come to hate the whole mechanism of answering machines, answering services, and secretaries and assistants who are also nearly mechanical. In protecting their time, the famous cavalierly take up huge chunks of yours. Yet, as angry and frustrated as I sometimes became, I couldn't resent too much being put off and shuffled around, for after all I was imposing on them.

So I tried to control my anger and remain persistent and cheerful, despite feeling like a beggar. Sometimes the effort to make contact was extended and complicated beyond belief, and there was nothing else to do but give up. Occasionally the process was so long I lost track of where I was in it, and occasionally the effort had been so great I found myself tongue-tied when *the* person did finally call.

On one of my later trips to New York, the attempts to get appointments with Elia Kazan, stage and screen director and more recently novelist, and Edward Albee, playwright (attempts which just happened to come at the same time), became so Byzantine that I began to think I was in a Kafka novel, an illusion reinforced by days of virtual imprisonment in a dark and dreary hotel room.

I had already spent three weeks in the city, interviewing and doing some work at the Pierpont Morgan and New York Public libraries, and then I began taking side trips to see people on Long Island and in Boston, Connecticut, and New Jersey, while all the time calling both gentlemen and trying to make arrangements for an interview that each, through Elaine, had already agreed to. I finally ran out of other things to do. Kazan had a secretary who seemed to be at her desk for about an hour sometime during the day every other day or so on an irregular and unpredictable basis. Most of the time the phone just rang, and I would sit there on the edge of the bed in my hotel room, trying to imagine where it was that the phone was ringing. Was this a completely empty office somewhere with a phone on the floor? When I did manage to catch her in, she would tell me to call back, that she knew Mr. Kazan wanted to see me.

In the meantime, I was waiting in the hotel room for Edward Albee to call. Staying in New York was costing me a fortune, money which had come out of the savings from a relatively meager salary. People who go to places like New York on business expense accounts have no idea, I suspect, what it is like to have to pay your own way, the anxiety involved. Every day at those prices made me more and more nervous.

During this kind of waiting, when what you are waiting for—in this case a return call from Albee—might come at any time, you can't leave the phone, and you can't give your attention to reading or writing. You are continually on edge. It is somewhat like waiting for company to come, and you are at loose ends, standing at the front window, staring at the driveway. The only daytime TV I could stand to watch was the noon news, and I dared not leave the room to eat until late in the evening. Of course, if I was out and he called, he could leave a message with the front desk, but that wouldn't do me any good. After ten days of this, I finally caught up to Kazan, but Albee's call never did come, and I was only able to get in touch with him years later in Los Angeles.

Kazan's office at that time was on Times Square in an old theater building that seemed largely deserted. It appeared to me that the office had become little more than a mail drop, since there was no one else there, and although there was furniture, it looked as if it had been unused for some time. The director-novelist is a short, dark, intense man, and quietly, unsmilingly, he invited me to come into a room, beyond the outer, small reception area, which contained a desk, chair, and couch.

The blinds were drawn, and under a small, dim light, Mr. Kazan lay down on what appeared to be a psychiatrist's couch, which complete nonplussed me for several minutes. I didn't know what my role should be but took my cue and let him talk. It turned out to be an excellent interview, worth waiting for. He had known Steinbeck well, not just socially but as a confidant of his hopes, problems, and disappointments.

Back in California, several weeks later, when I took the tape to my typist for transcription, she called to tell me that the tape was, after the first couple of minutes, blank. I couldn't believe it and felt like weeping. I still don't know what happened. It was the only such failure I had in hundreds of interviews. I can only guess that I might have reached out to adjust the position of the microphone and accidentally touched the on-off button just enough to cut it off.

I waited for a year or so and then wrote to Kazan, apologetically, to tell him what had happened. I asked for another interview, if he could possibly make the time. On my next trip to New York, after a miniature version of the delays and confusion I had experienced before, I went to see him, this time in an office in an old building on the West Side. I am sure that he didn't remember me from before, and I could see that he resented giving up the time and could hardly wait for me to leave. The result was what I had come to call a "yes, I knew him well" interview—cautious generalities that added up to nothing.

I blamed myself for muffing my first opportunity. Still, I wrote a note to him, thanking him profusely for taking the time to talk to me. Several years later, after the biography had come out, I got a letter from his secretary, asking why, in light of my letter of gratitude, I had not sent Mr. Kazan

Burgess Meredith as George and Lon Chaney, Jr., as Lennie in the film *Of Mice and Men*. Courtesy of Hal Roach Studios.

a copy of my book? Actually—and how could I tell her this?—I had been counting on people like her boss, who could afford the book, to buy it and help me come closer to breaking even.

The recording failure I had with Kazan was unusual, but I nearly went through the same thing with Burgess Meredith. Meredith had played the part of George in the film of Steinbeck's *Of Mice and Men* and had gotten to know John when the author visited the shooting of the film in the San Fernando Valley (the producer, Lewis Milestone, couldn't find a ranch that looked enough like the Salinas Valley in the Salinas Valley). He had been close to John during much

of the war, when the two were in London, and in the years
immediately after.

I was able to get Meredith's address from producer
Milestone, wrote to him, and with relatively little trouble
was able to arrange to meet him at his home in Malibu. The
house was down on the sand in a row of houses on a private
beach with a security gate and guard. When I arrived, he
was on the phone (famous people, like my daughters, are
always on the phone). I waited while he made several more
phone calls, a wait interrupted by the appearance of his
wife, a modishly slim blonde in a bikini, who at his introduction nodded vaguely in my direction on her way out to
the beach.

Meredith then told me that he had to go to the studio
and that he hoped I didn't mind talking to him on the way.
He had a sporty little yellow Mazda, comfortable, with air
conditioning, which was pleasant because it was a warm
day. I tried to put my mind to asking the right questions as
we zoomed down the coast highway and then inland toward
MGM. Talking to him was a bit unsettling, because, unlike
other celebrities I had talked to up to then, he was an actor
that I had seen on the screen dozens of times. I admired his
serious work, and my daughters had been addicted to the
"Batman" series on TV. When I told them I was going to
talk to the Penguin, they were, for the first time during my
project, suitably impressed.

Meredith talked animatedly and with great concentra-
tion, considering the traffic he had to deal with. I set my
tape recorder on the seat between us and held out the microphone with my hand. During the forty-minute trip, my
arm began to feel as if it was going to drop off, but there was
no place in the car to put the mike down. When we got to
the studio, he disappeared for most of three hours, as I
lounged about a large waiting room, with actors and studio
people coming in and going out.

Meredith and fellow cast members were being fitted for
costumes for a TV series and, as he told me later, being
photographed for publicity stills. A bonus came to me when

he rushed in for a moment with actor Kent Smith in tow. He had just found out that Smith had had the lead in the Broadway production of John's play *Burning Bright* and had come to know John fairly well. Grateful to Meredith, I got out my tape machine and recorded Smith's reminiscences.

I drove home that night to San Diego, and the next morning I began listening to the tape. The entire section which had recorded Meredith was almost entirely obscured by the sound of the air conditioner in his car blowing across the microphone that I had so laboriously held out toward him. But with a few cues from words that I could just barely make out over the whooshing noise, I was able to reconstruct from memory nearly everything that he had said. I found that recording any place but a rather quiet living room usually caused problems. On several occasions I was forced to interview in restaurants, and I always had difficulty hearing the tape, since someone hitting a dish with a fork ten feet behind you comes out clearer than speech directly into the mike from three feet away.

Despite a continuing underlying anxiety about calling up strangers and meeting new people, I discovered after several years of interviewing that, once I started talking to someone, I often enjoyed the process. Although it was a pain trying to get in touch with Arthur Miller, and difficult finding his house in rural Connecticut, I found it a joy to sit in his living room and talk to him and share a lunch he had cooked. He talked to me, I thought, as if he had known me all my life. And I must admit, after having taught his *Death of a Salesman* off and on for twenty years, I nearly swooned like any ordinary fan when, in talking about one of Steinbeck's problems, he casually commented that he supposed that "it comes with the territory." I was vulnerable too.

I came to realize that, for all my scorn of celebrity and celebrity worship, I was able, through the biography, to meet some pretty unusual people that I would never have otherwise had the opportunity to talk with. I liked talking with Miller so much that, as I left, I was saddened by the realization that I would never see or talk to him again. Such, too, was my feeling after talking with Burl Ives.

I arranged to interview the folk singer–actor at his home near Santa Barbara. After I was ushered into the large, tiled foyer of a Spanish-style mansion, the maid was showing me into the living room when a booming voice interrupted, calling down from upstairs, "If that's Professor Benson, send him up." (Even after two decades of college teaching, I was still startled when someone in the real world outside academe referred to me as "Professor Benson." Was that me?)

In an expansive bedroom that took up about half of the second story, I found Ives sitting up on an old-fashioned, canopied bed. The bed was very high off the floor, and on top of this platform sat Ives, surrounded by pillows, pitch pipes, and tape recorders, working on his music. He was dressed in an old-fashioned, ankle-length nightgown and tassled nightcap, so that with his white beard he looked something like Santa Claus, king of the mountain. As I approached, he looked down over his glasses at me and invited me to pull a chair up to the bed.

The interview was not only helpful but enjoyable and filled with laughter. After I had picked up my materials and thanked him, I paused near the door and said, "I'm sorry we won't see each other again." He waved at me from across the room and called out, "Don't worry, don't worry. We will certainly meet again in some other life."

When I got home, I played the interview for my wife, who for some years has been a fan of Ives—we have several of his records—and when it was over, she asked me, "Why didn't you ask him to sing?"

"How could I have done that?" I replied. She seemed genuinely disappointed.

There were some celebrity friends of Steinbeck, like Walter Cronkite, that I just gave up trying to see. I had taken so long to research the biography that I had to begin to weigh the benefits and possible information gained against the time and expense involved. In the case of Cronkite and several others, it seemed to me that their experience with John had been primarily social—at parties and such—and that their knowledge of him probably didn't run very deep.

And there were several others, like Fred Allen, whom I would have dearly loved to interview but who had died long before. A number of other people important in John's life were gone—Pascal Covici, his editor; Harold Guinzburg, his publisher; Frank Loesser, the composer and longtime friend; and, perhaps most important of all, John's younger sister, Mary. Most of those who were gone were men, however, and in almost every case they had left behind widows who were still alive. I interviewed the widows, but as helpful as they tried to be, it wasn't, of course, the same thing.

In one instance, I missed the boat, badly. Nunnally Johnson, the screenwriter who had done such a beautiful job in adapting *The Grapes of Wrath* to film, was still alive during the first few years that I was interviewing. However, I heard from several people that he was seriously ill with emphysema, spending much of his time in an oxygen tent. I felt that under the circumstances it would be very bad taste to bother him, to thrust myself into a situation that must be very difficult for him.

Several years after Johnson's death, someone mentioned that it might be helpful to me to interview his widow, so I made arrangements to see Dorris Johnson (who as Dorris Bowdon played Rose of Sharon in the film) in her home in Beverly Hills. She reported to me about several occasions when she and her husband and John and Gwyn had been together and was able to tell me some interesting things about the filming. She said it was a shame that I had not been able to talk to her husband. I told her that I never tried to get in touch with him because of his illness. "Oh," she said, "that's too bad. He was so lonely at times—he really longed for people to talk to during those last years."

8

Fear, Envy, and Loathing

The trouble with giving up trying to see some prospects is that you never know what you might be losing, and I felt that I was responsible for knowing just about everything. I also felt a certain historic duty—if I didn't take the time and effort to find out as much as I could, then, at least in regard to oral testimony, that information might well be lost forever.

But I was also accumulating a huge amount of material, and it was becoming increasingly difficult to handle and store. The scope of my job was wider than that of most other biographers because so very little had been known in any detail about John Steinbeck's life. He had been very private, not writing very much about himself and very seldom providing personal information on the few occasions he was willing to be interviewed. It was part of his credo that he did not want readers' knowledge of his life or consciousness of his personality to get in the way of seeing his work for what it was in itself. Nor did he want to become so well known that it became impossible for him to pass among ordinary people unrecognized. He finally gave up later in life on such things as not having his photograph taken, but he remained closemouthed about himself to the end.

So when I began my work, there was little knowledge of his life, and most of that very general and sometimes wrong, no biographies, and very few published letters, and in a sense nearly everything I discovered was new. As I proceeded, a thirst for material began to take over my consciousness—the more I learned, the more I needed to learn. More, more, more! I was like a forty-niner with a strike and no other miners around me. I didn't know whether I should grab every speck of paydirt in sight or more carefully survey the ground and concentrate only on chances for the largest nuggets.

With greed came the psychology of the miser. The material becomes yours. You alone have gathered it together, and you even keep it stored in a fireproof file that looks suspiciously like a safe. Of course, from the beginning I had worried about fire and other calamities. After my tapes were transcribed, I took them to the bank, where I had two large safe-deposit boxes. I became supercautious about fire, checking the stove, the fireplace, candles, or any ashtray where I had emptied my pipe, morning, night, and periodically during the day. We became the first family on our block to have smoke alarms, and I put fire extinguishers at strategic locations throughout the house. My wife looked at me as if I had gone off the deep end, but as I roamed the house sniffing for smoke and checking the windows, she merely shook her head and kept her own counsel.

I was also afraid of a break-in, not so much for theft as for vandalism. We had a couple of teenage kids in the neighborhood that we had caught stealing stuff out of our yard. In some strange, perverted way it was not we who held the grudge but they. They deeply resented our catching them, I suppose, and so for a couple of years we had fruit and rocks thrown against the house and every now and then an egg against the front door.

As we all know, there is nothing in today's society that can be done about such things, and so I waited and trembled, knowing that one day I would come home to an office where all the papers out of my files had been tossed together into a heap on the floor and mixed with fruit juice and catsup. It never happened. Not, I suspect, because they weren't capable of it, but because they didn't hate us quite enough to take the chance. Obscene gestures and catcalls every time they passed in front of the house, along with the fruit, eggs, and rocks, seemed to satisfy their sense of outrage. Since they kept this up for years, I have always wondered what revenge they would have been moved to had we really done something to hurt them.

Just as the miser never has enough money, so too the miserly biographer never has enough facts or anecdotes, never feels he knows enough yet to write. Later I would find that forcing myself to stop the research and start the writing of the manuscript brought on a crisis of the soul, like having to spend the gold that I had hidden.

Besides greed and miserliness, other unworthy emotions come into play when one discovers that there is competition. Fear, jealously, dislike approaching hatred—all emerged as possibilities, and I realized that I would have to struggle within myself to control and change these reactions or I would be eaten up on the inside. One can be so concerned about others and what they are doing that he is paralyzed.

For the most part, I felt I should do my own work and not worry about what others were doing—there was nothing I could do about them anyway. I had to force myself to realize that there would be many biographies of John Steinbeck and that my work would ultimately be only part of a process. There would be biographers after me who would use what I had discovered, add material of their own, and, indeed, find mistakes or omissions in my account, and they would come up with different, perhaps even more perceptive and valid, accounts of the life and work than mine. The problem was in part one of trying to suppress the ego and sense of self-importance.

I was helped in this struggle by the nature of the group of scholars I had joined, those who had devoted their energies largely to the study of Steinbeck. I have a theory, which may have a grain of truth in it, that in some way those who are attracted to the study of an author reflect that author's values or personality. Hemingway scholars seem to have a great gusto for good living and always seem to be able to schedule their conferences in Madrid or Paris. Faulkner scholars seem to be exclusive by inclination, aristocratic by taste. Their relations appear, at least to the outsider, often soured by backbiting and one-upmanship. By contrast, Steinbeck people seem relaxed and democratic and tend toward the slightly eccentric. A Steinbeck group is nearly always a quiet group, almost shy.

No one with driving academic ambition is going to pick Steinbeck to study, and that tends to eliminate the ego-maniacs and most of the internecine warfare of reputations that is typical among scholars. Instead, most Steinbeck scholars seem more focused on their subject than on themselves, usually standing together, cooperatively, against the slings and arrows of outsiders who may find their subject of dubious merit. I was fortunate, therefore, to get help and encouragement from nearly all quarters. Richard Astro, for example, who had started a biographical study of the Stein-beck–Ed Ricketts relationship before I began my work, could have greeted my entrance into the arena with hostility, but instead he provided leads, phone numbers, and copies of notes and papers. I, in turn, could do no less for him and asked my publisher to give his manuscript a read-ing—and so it went.

Outside the academic world, I quickly learned, was a writer who had started on a biography at just about the same time I had. He was Nelson Valjean, a former Salinas newspaperman and editor of Sunset Books, who was work-ing on his book as the major project of his retirement. I never met him, but we played tag all around California (his interest didn't extend beyond that because he was doing a biography of the "California years"). I would interview someone and shortly after learn that he had found the same person. Or I would go to talk to someone and find that Val-jean had just gone out the back door. For a time, it was very disconcerting. I didn't mind talking to the same people—that went both ways—but I did feel that I was acting as his bird dog, and I learned to watch what I said about other interviews to people I was interviewing.

As an example of the sort of thing that was happening, I got an idea from a neighbor, who at one time worked for the state fish and game depatment, to write to a retired administrator, Leo Shapovalov, who was working on a history of the department. The retired-official was very helpful, not only providing direct information about Steinbeck's employment with the department during the late 1920s but also supplying historic photos of the fish hatchery and leads to several former-employees who had known Steinbeck. Later, when Valjean's book came out, I found all the material that had originally come to me, the anecdotes and even the photos. How he located Shapovalov I don't know, but I suspect I must have mentioned my coup to someone who in turn passed it on to Valjean.

Still, the more I learned about Valjean, the more I came to respect him. By all reports he was a good and gentle man who had a real affection for Steinbeck and his work. Furthermore, he was working very hard and doing so under the burden of very poor health. He was confined to a wheelchair, and while he did make some visits in person, he was forced to do a lot of his interviewing over the phone. Nevertheless, he was persistent and exacting in his work, and was able to discover a lot of things on his own (I don't want to give the impression that all he did was track me) that would not have been discovered without his newspaperman's curiosity and eye for detail.

As I found out later, his illness was so severe that it was very difficult for him to write, let alone do research, yet he persisted. The biography kept him going, and in the end it was a race with approaching death—his book was published only a month before he died. When I read it, I was glad that it was a good book, one that will be of lasting interest (and one that several people have already stolen from, extensively). It is an entertaining account of John's early life, for, with the abandon of a nonacademic, Valjean tells some of the wildest and funniest stories about Steinbeck that are ever likely to reach print. Despite the pain, he must have had a good time writing it.

Over the years I heard of a number of other planned Steinbeck biographies. Every now and then I would see an announcement in the *New York Times Book Review* or the *New York Review of Books* by someone asking for information regarding Steinbeck for a projected biography, and my heart would sink a little bit. I don't know what happened to them—maybe they are still being written. A couple of publishers got in touch with me and, finding that I already had a contract, went out looking for their own biographers.

Little, Brown & Company was very persistent. First they lined up Nathaniel Benchley to do a biography of his old friend. But when Benchley found out from Elaine Steinbeck that she couldn't cooperate with him since she had already given her authorization to me, he dropped the project. Then I heard that Little, Brown had tried several other people, finally coming up with Thomas Kiernan, who had already done several biographies, including books on Yasser Arafat and Jane Fonda.

In the meantime, I learned that Elaine herself was planning to publish an edition of her husband's letters, and I felt that the rug was being pulled out from under me. I was grateful to Elaine for all her help and for standing by me with Benchley, but to publish the letters now, before the biography appeared rather than after, seemed to me to be preempting a good portion of the biography and negating a lot of my work. When a biography appears, one of the main questions that is always asked is, What is new? Now, nearly everything I had was new, but it wouldn't be for long. To make matters worse, the letters would be edited to make a more or less continuous narrative of John's life story (it was called *A Life in Letters*). It appeared as if Elaine had warded off Benchley only to mount a more deadly competition of her own.

The plan for the letters hit me very hard, and I skidded into a rather deep depression. I wrote to Elaine, trying to get her to postpone publication of the letters. I tried to point out that publication now would undercut me and that was why almost always in such situations the letters were released after the biography had appeared. But she was determined—she didn't even argue—and I was left to make the best of the situation. I had to do some work on my own thinking. After all, I told myself, Elaine is the literary heir, these are her husband's letters, and she can damn well do anything she pleases with them. She had given me so much, I'd better stop being so greedy. I didn't need everything to write a good book.

It seemed to me that I should do whatever I could to help her and her coeditor, Robert Wallsten, make the letter collection successful. I wrote them several long letters about experiences I had had with libraries, describing the procedures I had gone through and the protocol for obtaining material. This effort was probably superfluous, since the heir has complete access, and it became clear that they would not have to deal with the red tape that I had encountered. I also described for them collections I knew about, publicly held and private, and sent them an inventory of copies of letters I had. I could not send my notes taken from letters, because they would have been of no help, but by this time I did have a very large collection of photocopies. I copied them and sent them on, and in return Elaine sent me copies of letters that she had obtained on her own. When I got those, I was beginning to feel better and better about the whole thing.

But I got another jolt when the Kiernan book came out and I learned that he had got most of his material—access to the letters manuscript before publication—from Wallsten. Since I had contributed to that material, it was as if I had indirectly supplied research for a major competitor. I don't know of anyone besides Wallsten that Kiernan interviewed, and his library work seemed somewhat limited. The Stanford Library people told me that he had come in for two days and talked to the librarians. Carlton Sheffield, who had been Valjean's primary source, told me that Kiernan quoted him but that he had never laid eyes on the man.

Hell. Full speed ahead and damn the torpedoes.

"Do you think we can make it, skipper?"

"I don't know, but we're sure going to try, kid. Why don't

you go down and see if Smitty can't get a few more knots out of this old tub. . . . Oh, and while you're at it, see if they have that fire in the number two hold under control yet." A lot of my internal dialogue comes from B movies of the 1943–48 period that I saw at the El Rey Theatre instead of studying algebra.

What is a biography? What it meant to me at the time, I think, was working as hard as you can, to find out as much as you can. Maybe it is the story of a life by someone who hasn't lived that life and who therefore is likely to get it all wrong. Looking back, I like to think of it as a search for the truth, an attempt to construct a whole truth by intuition after having assembled a host of partial truths. There is an art, but it is not the art of fiction, which in biography is lying to cover your sloth or ignorance.

What a biography is not is an entertainment loosely based on selectively chosen facts. If you fictionalize historical characters, you are insulting the dead for reasons of ego or money. How many Roman or Greek leaders or warriors, English kings or noblemen do we know only, and falsely, through Shakespeare? We do not learn English history from Shakespeare, French history from Dumas, or American history from Kenneth Roberts. We learn history from history. Not that history is always true, but it is the intent that purifies. I think the dead do care and that they give us high marks for trying.

John Steinbeck's will, a life spent in pressing toward the secret heart of man and in segregating the true from the false, sat above the lintel of my office doorway. A dark, brooding spirit that wearily shook its head and mumbled, quoting T. S. Eliot, "That is not it at all, / That is not what I meant, at all."

What began as challenge, mystery, and excited discovery was, after nearly nine years of painstaking work, now a matter largely of frustration. There were always too many gaps, too little known, too few witnesses. It is an amazing thing how large a life is, particularly the life of someone like John Steinbeck. He was different from most of us not only because he was rich, which gave him more freedom and mobility, but because he was famous, which gave him wider acquaintance, and because he had an insatiable curiosity about people and places that drove him to a constantly active life. The letters he wrote, as more and more came to light, seemed to pile up indefinitely; the people he knew seemed to multiply endlessly; the places I should go—Mexico City, La Paz, London, Paris, Rome—even Moscow—stretched far beyond the limits of my checkbook.

For the last year and a half of my research, I worked to fill in as many gaps as I could. I interviewed new people, often those I had earlier passed over for one reason or another, and I went back to those I had already talked to with new questions. I went on and on, even after I started writing the manuscript, asking questions.

Some of the missing pieces were obvious, such as periods of a month or more for which I had no information, no clues about where John was or what he was doing. I was able to fill almost all of these gaps eventually, by going back and reexamining the bits of information I had (often it turned out that a letter was incorrectly dated or someone had given me a date from memory that was inaccurate) or asking questions of everybody I knew who had known John during that period.

Much of my time just before I started work on the manuscript and for several months after was devoted to trying to get a complete and accurate chronology. I had a good start on this from the work of an assistant during the first two years after I had decided to do the book as a biography. Barbara Hopfinger had been a graduate student of mine who had done her thesis on Steinbeck. She had finished her graduate work when she was in her early forties, and because of my own problems in the job market on account of my age, I had great sympathy for her situation—she was not only too old to start teaching (according to the "understood" criteria for college teachers) but also a woman, which made it even worse.

I knew she was bright, enthusiastic, and capable—I had

seen her teach and knew she was a damn good teacher—
and I felt keenly her disappointment and frustration when
she was unable to get a job. I wrote letters for her, called
people, and recommended a piece of her thesis for publication in a scholarly journal, but all to no avail. For a while,
she was able to get along by teaching part time, one composition class each at two different colleges; her only other
income was disability payments to her husband, who was ill
and retired at home. She volunteered to work for me at low
pay—all I could afford—to keep her hand in. She ended up
spending hundreds of hours preparing a basic chronology
for me on 5-by-8 cards, motivated primarily by her love of
Steinbeck's work.

Eventually she had to quit working for me and go to work
full time as a clerk-receptionist for the county. Her misfortune had been my good fortune, in that she did a very thorough job of asking the right questions, putting the pieces
together, excerpting the heart of an item or event. Now, at
the end of my years of research, I had to continue her work,
taking all that I had discovered since she left me, date it
and excerpt it, and file it in order with the other cards.

Beyond filling out the chronology, there were other gaps
that I was conscious of that worried me, although they
weren't as obvious. I was bothered by not having as thorough a sense as I should of what might be called the "negative view" of John generally held by Gwyn's side of the
family. I felt that John's two sons, probably owing to the influence of their mother, who largely reared them, seemed
to be very critical of him, and to be fair to them, and their
mother, I should try to get a greater exposure to their point
of view.

I had been in their company twice at Elaine's apartment,
but they were naturally restrained in their responses. Then
John IV came with Elaine one day to our home in La Mesa—
he had some close friends nearby—and he invited me to
stop by his friends' house while he was staying there so we
could talk. I called a week later and made arrangements to
go over in midmorning the next day. I arrived about 10:00

and was invited into the breakfast room to sit down and wait. For about an hour, I talked to the woman of the house, and then John's wife came in, and we talked for about an hour more. By this time, I was embarrassed and at a loss what to do. Then John came by the door to the hallway wrapped in a towel, grunted at me on the way by, and disappeared. After about twenty minutes more, I, in my dense way, got the message and left.

John IV, not really wanting to talk, had offered a "Great Gatsby" invitation. "We really ought to get together sometime for lunch" is its most obvious form, and I, like Gatsby, had rushed in to change my clothes. As for Thom, I tried repeatedly to locate him, but it was difficult, because I didn't want to do it through his stepmother, and no one else, even Gwyn, seemed quite sure where he was. The only other possible source for this point of view was Gwyn's mother.

I knew from the letters that John, Sr., had disliked her so intensely and thought her such a bad influence on his marriage that he refused to see her for nearly a year and thereafter only rarely. My impression, even from Gwyn, was that she was dogmatic, demanding, and narrow-minded. Nevertheless, I thought I should talk to her, and so I called and talked to her husband, Stanley Heuit, and asked for an interview. Two days later he called back, and we made an appointment. I flew to Tucson and then drove a hundred miles south to Nogales, which is split into two towns on the Mexican border. The house was several miles out from the center of town in a tract of two-bedroom, white-stucco bungalows. The heat and brightness of the sun hit me as I got out of my air-conditioned rental car, and I walked up the front path reluctantly. I just wanted to get it over with.

I knew that Mrs. Heuit was quite elderly, and I was surprised when I was greeted at the door by a good-looking man who appeared to be in his late fifties or early sixties. As I was ushered through the small living room, I was startled to run into a huge painting of Gwyn on the wall. It was a glamorous pose—in a low-cut evening dress, she sat, lean-

A painting of Gwyn Steinbeck which once hung in the Heuit home.
Courtesy of the Steinbeck Research Center, San Jose State University,
San Jose, California.

ing with one arm nonchalantly on the back of a wooden chair. Her blonde hair, curled in the manner of the early 1940s, framed a pale, pretty face that seemed almost completely devoid of expression. The lack of expression was startling—as if there were no one in the body. The painting was too large for the wall, too large for the room, and seemed to dominate the house, as if the house and the people in it were there only to pay homage to the painting.

In a small bedroom in the rear, Mrs. Heuit lay on a hospital bed, adjusted so that she partly sat up. All the surfaces in the crowded room were filled with bottles, small boxes, and appliances that seemed evenly divided between makeup and medication. I had heard that she was in her late eighties, but although her body and hands looked very fragile and old, her face, through either a fairly recent face-lift or the nature of her illness, was unlined, the skin tight. Her skull almost showed through the white, nearly translucent skin, and the rouge and bright-red lipstick gleamed in shocking contrast. I was touched by the effort I assumed she had made on my behalf to present herself, yet as a contradiction to her effort, I found that I had to move a bed pan, among other appliances, from the chair when she asked me to sit down.

Although I did ask some questions, she went on for the most part without any prompting. I am certain that she had reviewed, perhaps even practiced, what she was going to say to me. It was as if I were recording a last testament, a message of venom and vengeance. Her intensity was frightening. John's nickname for her had been "Birdeyes," and the name took on a new meaning for me as those bright, penetrating eyes fixed me. She held me with those eyes the way someone might grab you by the arm to detain you, a strong grip that makes you just want to get away somehow.

I felt certain that she hated John Steinbeck, despised him. Gwyn had been her hope, and she apparently really had believed that her daughter would become a star. But John had ruined all that. He was uncouth, lower-class, as anyone could see from the bums he associated with and the language he used in his books. He was sloppy and careless in the way he lived and neurotic in his fear of people and publicity.

He was a coward: "I don't mind saying he was a natural-born coward, and he always carried guns. He was scared all the time, running scared. I think mostly after *The Grapes of Wrath*, because a lot of people he wrote about he went to school with, and they were out to get his hide because it cost them a lot of money to have to change the mode of living of the itinerant workers." He was jealous: "Terribly jealous—he was jealous of his own children. He was jealous of his own dog. I can't explain to you the man's jealousy." He was foul-mouthed: "About as foul-mouthed as you can get—and without a doubt, he was the wickedest man I ever encountered in my life."

Unlike her daughter Gwyn, who had seemed to me to make some things up, whole cloth, she simply colored things that actually happened with her hatred. She told me story after story that demonstrated John's ineptitude, drunkenness, or vulgarity. I ended up using three of her stories, after checking with other sources and after trying to wash away the toxic additives. I felt that they brought a needed dimension to the portrait in truth that I was trying to paint.

Mrs. Heuit went on in a strong, clear voice with gritty determination for almost an hour and a half. Then she stopped, as suddenly and definitely as she had begun. I thanked her and bid her good-bye, but she didn't seem to know that I was there. The bright eyes had become dull and vacant. Her husband, who the whole time had hovered in the background, occasionally interrupting with medicine or a phone message, ushered me to the door. He was obviously relieved to see me go.

I had roamed the country and had learned what it meant for the traveling salesman to stay in one Holiday Inn after another and be delayed at one airport after another. I discovered what it felt like to have your baggage, along with your professional tools, lost, and I figured out how to wash and dry my shirts and underwear in a motel room. I learned to deal with indigestion and the threat that in the middle of an interview, I might be hit with an attack of diarrhea. And I had to learn all over again how to sleep with doors slamming (the college dormitory), babies crying (young parenthood), and loud parties extending into the early morning (apartment living).

I had become familiar with all the other noises of the night in a hotel or motel—the ice machine dumping its load, the coke machine dropping its cans or making change, the elevator starting and stopping, and the startling rattle at three in the morning by someone trying to unlock my door.

I had been lost in Boston while driving a car in heavy traffic, unable to stop or ask directions, and I had been stuck in the snow in New York. I had taken the very plane from Saint Louis to Carbondale, Illinois, that later had crashed, putting Air Illinois out of business. I had rented a car that, as I drove around the hills behind Santa Cruz looking for a house without an address, stalled and quit every time I started up a grade. I left my glasses on a plane—they had fallen out of my coat pocket in the overhead luggage compartment.

Disaster even struck close to home. On my way back from a long trip, weary and yearning for my own bed, my car quit on a San Diego freeway, and I sat there, with my emergency lights blinking, from 9:00 P.M. to 2:30 A.M., when my wife finally found me. I had tried to climb the fence but couldn't get over the barbed wire, and so I watched nine highway patrol cars go by and five city police and sheriff cars as I blinked my headlights, waved, and screamed.

Now that all of my wandering and adventures were largely over, I found myself more and more confined to my office at home, a space roughly 11 by 7 feet. What room there was to move around was nearly filled with my desk and filing cabinets, and when I was looking for something, which was most of the time, all the open floor was covered with file folders, papers, and books. Walking across the room was like tiptoeing across on the rocks of a creek bed. On my desk was my trusty old German portable, which I used throughout the project, hammering it so hard that it repeatedly simply fell to pieces. But I was able to find an old-country repairman who loved these typewriters so much he was willing to make the parts that were no longer available.

I began the manuscript with very grandiose plans. I wanted not just to write an ordinary biography but also to create a new art form. Like so many who had gotten into trouble before me, I was inspired by John Dos Passos's technique in *U.S.A.*, where he interspersed various materials—newspaper headlines, popular-song fragments, and small biographies—into his narrative. My idea was to insert, first, newspaper reports into my narrative. The old *Salinas Index* had reported John's birth and periodically had noted the family's activities. Later, of course, I could use pieces from *Time* and the *New York Times*, announcing books, trips, and marriages. Second, I was going to use, in the manner of Dos Passos, songs, newspaper reports of significant local and national events, and excerpts from government reports to give the flavor of the times. And third, I was going to insert brief biographies of those close to Steinbeck who influenced the course of his life.

I followed this plan as I traced John's life and times through his childhood into young adulthood and ended up with 360 pages. It became quite clear to me that I would never get through his life at that rate, and so I rewrote, leaving out all the extra material and also cutting down on the anecdotes, and I wound up with 57 pages. But that was what led me to make one of the stupidest mistakes in the book. John's date of birth was announced in one of the newspaper bits that I took out, and somehow the date of birth never got back in.

I was glad that I got rid of my ambitious plan, because it seemed to me that it was too devoted to a virtuoso performance by me—I wanted to show off John, not show off myself. The best book, I felt at this point, would be one in which the reader thought always of John Steinbeck, without being conscious of the writer telling them the story. This concern, plus the problem of length, was what led me to decide early not to devote space to an evaluation and discussion of John's works—it would be enough just to get down the story of his life, completely and accurately, for the first time.

Earlier I had done quite a bit of work on Hemingway, publishing a book and editing two volumes of criticism, and I had learned a great deal from him about writing. One of my creative-writing teachers in college had told us about Hemingway's constant revision, that he would rewrite something thirty, forty, or even fifty times (later I learned that this story was largely a myth). I was so impressed by Hemingway's persistence that I began the habit of revising everything I wrote, over and over. When you don't have enormous talent and what you write usually doesn't come out very well, this practice gives you hope that, with enough work and determination, you can eventually come up with something that is fairly decent. And I have always had more determination than talent.

I may be the only professor of English in the United States so insecure about his writing that he revises his letters to his mother. Over the years I have developed a technique that is very time-consuming but seems to work. I start by composing a paragraph (I use the typewriter); then as I go on to a second paragraph, I go back and rewrite the previous one. When I have a section of three or four pages, I start over again. Eventually I have a chapter, and I go back and rewrite the entire chapter. If the chapter doesn't come out right, I pull it to pieces, save some pieces, discard others, and write the chapter again. Actually, when I write, I do more typing than anything else.

Another thing I learned from Hemingway was always to leave something in the tank for the next day. Don't write yourself out, but keep for the next writing session some of the ideas and the enthusiasm for getting them down on paper. Otherwise, you will get up in the morning, sit down at the typewriter, and spend half a day wondering where you are going to go next. That sense of complete blankness and bewilderment seems to come often enough by itself without encouraging it. When I got stuck, I would read the previous portion over and over, hoping to generate enough juice to get going again.

When that didn't work, I would read through my notes and look over the chronology file. My remedy of last resort was to go out into the yard (a year-round possibility in San Diego) and do physical labor of some kind, the nastier the better. The stimulation that comes after a half hour of weeding or turning over sod or mixing concrete is amazing—particularly if it is uncomfortably hot or cold outside. The thoughts just come flooding into the mind. It must be some automatic escape mechanism in the cortex.

One thing I didn't take from Hemingway was his style, which is far too showy and self-conscious. I wanted to write the manuscript in as natural-sounding prose as I could manage, trying to fit the words and rhythm to the content and avoiding as much as possible the stilted language of the academic. I wanted to avoid any tricks that would call atention to themselves—no figure skating with lifts, leaps, and spins. I hoped for some gracefulness, but, frankly, I just wanted to write well enough that no one would complain.

I was worried that after all the work I had done the manuscript might be rejected. I had always hoped that Viking, Steinbeck's publisher, would take the book. Getting permissions would be made a lot easier, and there was always a chance, since Steinbeck was one of Viking's star authors, that the publisher would make an extra effort to merchandise the book. At first, Tom Guinzburg, the son of Steinbeck's publisher and now president of Viking, wanted the book and took an option on it, but he later changed his mind, saying that he had decided a publisher should not publish a biography about one of its own authors. Then Viking was sold to Penguin, and the new managing editor, Alan Williams, decided that Viking should do the book after all. But the commitment seemed to me to be very tentative, and I was worried that the manuscript might be rejected. Indeed, in the back of my mind was the nagging fear that no one would take it, that it wouldn't be good enough to find a publisher.

The time I was taking began to weigh very heavily on me. Through Elaine I got inquiries from people in Sag Harbor that I had interviewed years earlier: When could they see the book? I got notes and phone calls from sources in the Salinas-Monterey area wanting to know when the book would be done—surely, they implied, you must have had enough time by now. Although nothing was said directly, I felt some impatience in Elaine, my agents, and Viking. Friends had become bored with the whole thing and no longer asked how the book was coming along—which was fine with me—and "the project" became a sort of academic joke at work—you know, the professor who is always working on the big book which is somehow never completed.

I love the story about John, who, when he got tired of the pressure of friends in later years, would pass a card to them, without comment, which simply said, "I wrote 2,000 words today."

After a year of trying to grab every spare minute of every day, letting the house, yard, and car go to hell, and still not making much progress, I knew that I'd have to get some time off from teaching, somehow. I was reluctant to take a sabbatical, since the last time I had done that I had had to borrow money to make up the difference between the half pay of sabbatical and my regular salary, and it had taken us five years to pay off the loan. But I was able to get a fellowship from the National Endowment for the Humanities for a year, and then when Viking came through with an advance, I was able also to take a sabbatical. Without those two years devoted almost entirely to writing, it would have taken me at least three years longer.

Finally, the day came, in 1981, after about three and a half years of writing, that the manuscript was finished. Over the last eight months I had pushed myself as hard as possible in a final sprint to reach the finish line. I was exhausted but exhilarated. I had done it—and I had never really been quite sure that I could. Then in my exhilaration and to complete that push that was still in me to get the manuscript to the publisher, I did a really stupid thing: I packed up the manuscript in five boxes and sent each one off by express mail, at twenty-five dollars a box.

The reason spending the money was so stupid was that the books sat at Viking month after month, unread. I realize now, after reading magazines in which writers compare notes, that the relationship between writer and publisher is a very peculiar one. You would think that the same customs that govern the communications between friends or colleagues would apply, but they don't. There isn't even a business relationship. The closest I can come to describing it is a combination of a welfare recipient dealing with government bureaucracy and a child dealing with an absent-minded and noncommittal parent.

After sending my manuscript in a rush by overnight express, I expected within the first week or two some sort of letter saying: "We have received your manuscript, and we will read it and give you our opinion as soon as possible. Since it is very long, this may take us some time." However, weeks went by without any word whatsoever—I didn't even know whether or not they had received the manuscript. I was very hesitant to say anything—I certainly didn't want to antagonize anyone—but after three months I wrote to ask.

I got a reply that they had received it. I waited another four months and then asked, Was anyone reading it? I got a letter from Williams telling me that he had wanted to edit the book himself but he had been so busy he had decided to give the project over to another editor. The editor was William Strachan, who was new to Viking. I knew that it would take Strachan some time to get settled into a new job, and so I waited again for several months. Then I wrote again, and again, over a two- or three-month period, but without any reply. It had been, now, about a year and a half, and the anxiety had been building—were they not answering because they thought it was terrible and they couldn't decide what to do?

9

Looking for Steinbeck's Ghost

Research and writing have their frustrations, but the most difficult part of being a writer is the waiting. It is part of the pattern of supply and demand, I suppose, that, since there are a great many more writers than there is need for their work, editors of books and periodicals demand that an author respond, revise, or proofread immediately, while they will let the author rot on the vine weeks or months without notifying him what the status of his work may be. But if one reads the letters of writers a hundred years ago or two hundred years ago, he finds evidence that this has always been so—an essayist in London might wait two or three years before getting any word at all from a magazine or journal editor.

For me, as for most other writers, the arrival of the mail became the major event of every day. Emily Dickinson wrote of hope as "the thing with feathers," but my hope came in a red, white, and blue jeep. Rain or shine, I would rush out with my insides in a turmoil, reach into the box, and impatiently thumb through the catalogs, bills, and contest announcements. No lover ever waited more patiently or passionately for his scented envelope and the words he longed for than I, as I waited to see those large block letters in the upper-left-hand corner of an envelope: THE VIKING PRESS. Perhaps inside it would say, "We love your manuscript."

When the mailman was late, I fretted and paced, unable to do much of anything until he arrived. Then two months into my waiting period, the mail, which had been coming in the late morning for years, began to come regularly an hour later. Every few weeks the mail time changed, getting

later and later, until finally we began to get it at 4:00 and
4:30 in the afternoon. These increasing delays were doing
much to spoil the quality of my life. I called the post office
to complain. I was told that they were doing everything
possible to correct the problem—a typical government answer that meant nothing. I asked the postman, and he
could only grumble that "a new postmaster downtown was
screwing everything up." I could only reflect on how important to me such a small thing had become and how helpless I was to deal with it.

I never did get any kind of formal acceptance. Instead,
after six months of waiting, there was an expression of admiration for the work I had done from my new editor, Bill
Strachan, and a request that I shorten the manuscript. It
was like suddenly getting married without any courtship. I
knew that the length would be a problem, but I didn't feel
that while I was writing that should be uppermost in my
mind. I made my decisions to include or not include material depending on whether I felt it was important to the
story. The story would find its own length.

All at once, however, length became a big issue. My
agents were adamant that the manuscript must be cut se-
verely; Elaine thought it should be cut, advising that she
had felt that her edition of the letters had not sold as well as
it might have because of its size. Viking warned that the
book would be too expensive and too intimidating. I knew
that these things might be true and that chances for good
reviews (very long books irritate the hell out of time-pressed
reviewers—as an occasional reviewer, I know the feeling
when you get a four-pound book in the mail) and a book-
club adoption would be in jeopardy. But I also knew that I
hadn't spent all this time and effort to try to make money
and that I would get only one chance to do it the way it
should be done—I didn't have enough life left to mount
such effort again.

I took my stand, which was that I would cut to make the
book better (not more salable or immediately attractive)
but would not cut just to make it shorter. My decision was

based in part on two examples I had before me of other biographies. Carlos Baker's biography, *Ernest Hemingway: A Life Story*, seemed to me too short. Baker is an excellent writer, but there is no way anyone could jam Hemingway's event-filled life into 564 pages and cover the ground without sacrificing some readability. Baker does as well as anyone could, getting an enormous amount of information down, gracefully, on each page. Joseph Blotner's *Faulkner: A Biography* seemed to go in the opposite direction, too long for the story. Blotner has shown in other works that he is also a good writer, but he seems to be in such awe of the "great man" that he feels compelled to include *everything*.

According to Gore Vidal, among others, the length of a biography should depend on the relative greatness of the author, and in an article in the *New York Review of Books*, he mourns that so many pages should have been given to such "minor" writers as Ernest Hemingway. Vidal may come out with a length guide for biographers: 700 pages for Edmund Wilson, 650 for Evelyn Waugh, 200 for Hemingway, 100 for Steinbeck, and one wonders how many for Vidal. But I don't think a literary biography is a tribute or a monument. It is a work of art, with its proportions and relations among parts dictated by the nature of the story itself and the effect that the artist is trying to achieve. To assign an arbitrary length to a biography is like ordering a painting to match the decor of a house.

The request to shorten the manuscript meant further delay, and so I attacked the job with the same zeal I had shown when I finished the manuscript in a flurry and sent it off by express. Among other motives, I was beginning to worry about my flanks. I had already been scooped twice, and I thought that someone might come out of nowhere with yet another biography and saturate the market and defuse everyone's curiosity before I could get on the scene. When the manuscript was sitting at Viking, I was helpless to get things moving, but now it was in my hands, and I worked around the clock with every bit of energy I could find. I went through the material as ruthlessly as I could,

cutting paragraphs, pages, whole sections of chapters. Anything that seemed weak or superfluous, anything about
which I had any doubt at all, was crossed out. The manuscript was a patchwork of cuts, pastes, and new transitions.
It looked so bad that Bill and I considered having it re-
typed, although the clean copy had cost me $2,200 to have
typed the first time—and that was at bargain rates by a typist who felt sorry for me.

In about three weeks I had done the cutting and sent it
off (by regular mail—insured). I waited for some word. In
the back of my mind, along with worries about competition
and sagging personal finances, I was still concerned that
Viking might dump the whole thing as unprofitable, paying
off my contract with a token fee that might cover my hair-
cuts for a year. So I was back to ordering my day around the
arrival of the mailman. After two months, I couldn't stand it
anymore, and I wrote to ask what was happening. Did they
approve of the changes? Was there now a publication schedule? Finally, I got a letter back from Bill saying that the reason he hadn't written was that he had had nothing to tell
me. That was not very reassuring.

Then, what seemed like years after the original submission, but which was probably no more than two, Bill and I
started another round of cutting. This time we went through
the manuscript word by word, line by line, and Bill did
some editing as well as sending me, chapter by chapter,
suggested cuts and changes. This went on for four months,
back and forth in the mail and a number of conversations
over the phone to New York. Following this, there was another period of waiting of three months, and the copy editing began. At this stage I began to feel that Viking might
really take the book after all.

The one thing that I had asked for, from the beginning,
was a good copy editor. I had learned from other publishing
experiences that an able and discriminating copy editor can
make all the difference between a book that is well done
and one that you can be ashamed of. A good copy editor is
one that is particular without being petty, who can not only

catch the bloopers and obvious errors but detect the subtle contradictions and inadvertent omissions. Above all he is someone who has some sympathy for your prose style. William Faulkner accused Random House of always assigning him English majors just out of Vassar who were bound and determined to teach him how to write and punctuate properly.

I was not in the same league as Faulkner, but I knew how he felt when I got my edited copy back from Viking. Almost every sentence had been altered. It wasn't that I had made mistake after mistake, but that she (I assumed it was a she from the handwriting) didn't like the way I wrote and thought she could do better. Maybe she could, but damnit, she could write her own book, not rewrite mine. The changes began with the very first sentence. I had begun, "Just as his father would get on his horse and ride off to be alone, John Steinbeck had to get away from his house, from his family. Perhaps it was this impulse to get away that brought him so close to nature so young."

Now those sentences may not look like much, but it took me a week of writing, considering, and trying out various possibilities to get what I wanted. The first sentences are the most important in the book—that's when the reader can stop without making a commitment of time and effort. In these I thought I had pulled the reader in with the right rhythm and the hint of mystery. My copy editor had rewritten the first sentence something like this: "John Steinbeck, like his father, needed to get away from his family to be alone." The sentence didn't even make sense. No longer was I worried about publication or impatient about lost time. At first, I was so sick to my stomach I couldn't function, and then, I was just plain angry—really angry. The more I read, the more stupid, needless changes of style I saw, and by the time I had gone through the manuscript, I knew I would rather not publish the book at all than publish it in such a condition.

I sent indignant letters to Bill, even more indignant than they might have been, since I thought I had been promised veto power over the choice of copy editor based on a trial of one or two chapters. What had been mangled had been nearly the whole manuscript, and Viking was reluctant to change. It was only after the publisher had consulted with my agents, who were also agents for the Steinbeck estate, and the agents expressed an opinion that the copy editing was outrageous, that the way was cleared for us to start all over again with a new copy editor. This editing went to the other extreme and ignored too many outright errors (as I found out later in some detail—after publication, I had four complete strangers send me lists of typos and grammatical goofs; perhaps this is their hobby), but I knew that after one fight I had used up what little credit I had and made the best of it.

At this point, more than two years had gone by. I had worked over the manuscript, counting the three reviews with the typist before the original submission, seven times. I had it practically memorized, but I was so sick of my own prose that nothing sounded right. Nearly anyone can write competently if he works hard enough at it, but to write well, you need to take some risks. You need to depart from the pattern, from the expected, and do some things in your prose that might subject you to complaint or ridicule. Now as I looked at such places in the manuscript, I felt foolish and self-conscious. I didn't like the book very much, I was tired, and I just wanted it all over with. Viking had at last announced a publication date of July 1, 1983. I couldn't imagine a worse time for a book publication, but I didn't care. Dreams of glory were gone. I just wanted to get the damn thing into print and have it all behind me.

About the time the manuscript went into the editing process, I took my last trip to New York. I wanted to go over the photographs with the editor, Bill Strachan, and talk to him about selection and their location in the finished book. It seemed to me that since Steinbeck had been intimately connected with his environment, wherever he had lived, I should express that connection with pictures in the biogra-

phy. I had even gone so far as to ask an old friend and professional photographer, Dick Allman, to take some pictures
of John's houses and locations that might be associated with
his novels.

Beyond seeing Bill, I also wanted to go over the manuscript with Elaine—she had made a list of items that she
questioned or that seemed to her inaccurate in some way—
and I wanted to go up to the Sag Harbor house to take some
photographs. I was no photographer, and I would rather
have had Dick go, but there was no way I could afford to
bring him from California. He had already taken photographs in various locations in "Steinbeck Country," paying
his own expenses in the hope of recovering them after the
book was published, and I was embarrassed to ask him to
do more.

After spending most of a day with Bill, I made arrangements with Elaine to spend the weekend by myself in her
house at Sag Harbor. To tell the truth, I wanted not only to
take some pictures but also to spend some time alone in
John's house and garden, to think and perhaps—there is no
other way to put it—to make some kind of final peace with
John's spirit. I had known all along that he didn't like what I
was doing—he had in life frequently expressed antipathy
toward some future biographer "mucking around in his private affairs"—and I think I had some idea of going up there
to make some kind of gesture of expiation. It was all very
vague in my mind, but I was impelled, for whatever reason, to go.

Rainy, windy, and cold, it was a weekend designed for
lonely meditation and confronting ghosts. Dick Olmstead,
whom I had so unsuccessfully interviewed years earlier,
had kindly agreed to take me to the house and back to the
train station, and he met me dressed in a yellow slicker and
driving his four-wheel-drive truck. He mentioned that the
next evening, Saturday, some people were getting together
at Bob Barry's Marina and that I was welcome to drop by. I
thanked him and said maybe I would, but I had come up to
be alone and think about John.

It was getting dark as I grabbed my bag and dashed from the car through the wind-driven blasts of rain to the rear door of the Steinbeck house and tried to fit the key. Once I was in, I reached out to locate a light switch, always a tricky proposition in jury-rigged vacation homes, and then, finding one switch in the kitchen, I went through the house turning on lights, trying to make a strange place more friendly. I stashed my suitcase in the bedroom, washed my face and hands, and then sat down in what had been John's chair in the little sitting room next to the kitchen. Suddenly I had run out of things to do. I thought for a moment and realized I was hungry and almost automatically went into the kitchen, checking out the refrigerator and the cupboards, one after another. There was plenty of food, but I realized that none of it was mine, and I didn't think I should eat any of it. I was sorely tempted by a box of frozen breakfast rolls that had a delicious picture on the box, but what if I couldn't find a replacement at the grocery story in town and Elaine's sister and her boyfriend came in early some morning expecting to eat? The vividness of their indignation sent me back into the sitting room.

I watched the news on TV and again ran out of things to do. I decided that, if I was going to eat, I was going to have to hike into town. The only problem was that I wasn't quite sure where town was—somewhere to the west—or how to get there. Nevertheless, it was a problem I could work on, and I located a flashlight and an old raincoat and took off in the rain and the dark looking for Sag Harbor. Even in the limited visibility, there was something of a glow in the distance which I took to be the town, and I worked my way in that direction, hitting first a couple of dead-end roads that made me backtrack. After fifteen minutes of this, I began to get alarmed at the prospect of never finding my way back to the house.

At last I found a main road going in the right direction, and after first checking the signs at the intersection so I would know where to turn coming back, I walked about two miles into town. No one else was on Main Street, and when I stopped in at a restaurant that Elaine, years earlier, had pointed out to me as being one that John had frequented, I found it nearly as deserted as the house that I had just come from. It was a long, slow dinner, and I had four cups of coffee afterward, putting off the wet walk home.

Back at the house, I stripped down and took a bath, which was a strange experience because I had not had a tub bath since I was a child and because this was the tub that John had soaked in by the hour when he felt down or out of sorts. I had some trouble figuring out the plumbing on the tub and also getting in and out, since it was large and stood high off the floor. By the time I got to bed and turned off the light and lay listening to the rain on the windows and the tree branches on the roof, I had decided that what I was doing was a stupid, if not downright ghoulish, thing. Why had I come here?

I got up the next morning early, after a fitful night of strange sounds and unpleasant dreams, only one of which I could remember: I was in a strange hotel in a strange city, and I kept going up and down the elevator and back and forth in the hallways looking for my room. Awake and in the kitchen, I was once more tempted by the beautiful picture on those breakfast rolls but forced myself to settle for coffee; not finding any coffee, I had a cup of tea. I looked outside. It was one of those days with big thunderous-looking clouds floating majestically across the sky—very "formal weather" John had called it in one of his letters—raining part of the time and clearing part of the time. I spent much of the morning taking pictures and nosing about, exploring just about every inch of ground and then stopping to sit, during a rain shower, on John's boat dock, looking out over the choppy water of the cove.

By the time I got up to go in, I was feeling mournful again and a little bit guilty, so I decided to walk into town and have breakfast or lunch, whatever it was time for. I went back to John's coffee shop and had a breakfast at lunchtime and then took a walking tour of the town, stopping in at the grocery store where John had shopped and which he

Long Wharf, Sag Harbor, 1980. Photograph by the author.

had used in *Winter of Our Discontent* and going on to the
wharf and the various marinas. I looked at the boats and the
gulls, took some pictures, and then went back up Main
Street to the bar that John had frequented and had beer by
myself in a corner. By this time it was late afternoon, and I
found another restaurant that Elaine had mentioned and
ordered dinner. It was obviously off season, and in the restaurant they didn't know quite what to do with me alone
and early but managed to scrape together a good fish dinner. I stopped at a little gift shop on the way back, also deserted, and bought my wife a necklace with a whale woven
out of brass wire. The purchase made me feel better, and I
got home just before dark.

I spent the evening looking through the bookcase at
John's books. The only thing I could find to climb on to

Joyous Garde, at Bluff Point, 1980. Photograph by the author.

reach the top shelves was a rickety barstool that swiveled. I
almost broke my neck three or four times falling off before I
decided to call it an evening and went to bed.

The next morning I felt tired of walking and decided to
give up eating until I got back to the city that night. I had
had enough sense, however, to buy a little jar of instant coffee at the grocery store. It was overcast and cold, but I took
my coffee outside and sat under the English oaks that John
had planted. It was quiet all around me, and I sat listening
to the silence and waiting for something. After a time, I got
the key from the house and walked down to the little six-
sided house that John had built to do his writing in, "Joyous
Garde." I felt a little like a burglar as I took off the padlock,
went in, and raised the blinds on two or three of the windows that overlooked the cove.

I sat for a long time looking around me at John's things. Years ago when Elaine had first shown me the place, she had explained that she kept it pretty much as John had left it because people expected it to be preserved in that way. So his pencils were sharpened and sat, points up, in a pencil stand; yellow writing pads, some partly used, lay around on the desk here and there, and off to one side were boxes of clips and rubber bands ready for use. On the walls were clipboards and spring clips to hold memos, little shelves, and accordion envelopes, and above the windows was a shelf that held the books that he had been using in his last years.

But there was no sense of John here either. It was obvious, despite the casual clutter, that he had been gone a long time. The rubber bands, some cut from inner tubes, had begun to crack and change color; the clamps on the clipboards were beginning to rust, as was a pair of dog nail clippers hanging from a hook; the blotter on the writing desk, an adjustable drawing board, was dusty and had grown brittle. The pencils, all sharp, sat up at the ready, but the wood around the lead had aged and turned dark. No one would ever use them, and it suddenly came to me that I was being very silly, sitting here in this decaying relic, a house that no longer had any function.

By the time Dick came to pick me up to take me back to the train station, I had figured it out—that whatever was left of John was in his books and in the thoughts of the living, those who had known him. Although I thought I knew him by now, I would never really touch him except, vicariously, through them. In the front seat of the truck, Dick turned to me and said, "We missed you last night. All of us that had known John got together so we could compare stories for you." I had forgotten all about his invitation, and I felt like hell thinking about all those people waiting for me to show up.

I woke up Tuesday morning, the morning I was supposed to see Elaine, in my Manhattan hotel room and got up and looked out the window. Everything was white. My God, it was April! I couldn't believe it. I turned on the local TV news and found tht they were already calling it the spring blizzard of the century. All surface transportation—buses, taxis, and cars—was stopped, and the camera panned over a paralyzed city. Since I couldn't get to Mrs. Steinbeck's by subway, I'd have to walk. Her schedule was usually full, and to try to postpone our discussion of the manuscript even one day might mean that I'd have to come back to New York on yet another trip.

I was prepared for rain, but hadn't even thought of snow, so I did what I could to keep warm—I figured I had about forty-five blocks to walk. I put on two T-shirts, a long-sleeved shirt, a lightweight sweater, and my tweed sports jacket. Over all this I wore my thin raincoat, and having noticed people in the street carrying umbrellas (something I would not have thought to use in a snowstorm), I carried that along too. When I got outside, I found that it was very windy and a lot colder than I had thought it would be. I was plenty warm in the center, but I had had enough experience with the pain of frostbite to be worried about my ears, hands, and toes. So as I walked crosstown, I looked for a place where I might improve my winter wardrobe, and on the East Side, I ran into Bloomingdale's.

I made my way through the overheated store to the men's department and located the gloves by a mob standing around a table. Nearly all the gloves were gone, but I managed to find a pair of medium, fleece-lined driving gloves at an outrageous price (presumably I was dealing with the real thing here and not a vinyl imitation). Next I asked for and found the stocking caps and grabbed the last one while two men stood making up their minds. Then I went to the shoe department and asked for galoshes. All they had were those dress galoshes that barely cover the soles of your shoes, but better those than wet feet. I tried at Bloomingdale's and then at two shoe stores to find wool socks and finally had to settle for putting on an extra pair of summer-weight socks. I was ready.

I faced the wind with determination and headed toward
the upper East Side along Lexington Avenue. Street crews
were out, the taxis were trying to function, and people,
bent over against the wind, were fighting to keep their umbrellas from collapsing. Everyone in New York, man or
woman, wears a black coat and carries a black umbrella.
They seem to think that colors in such things are a mark of
weak-kneed, tropical character. I had on a brown-plaid
London Fog and stood out from the natives like a naval officer in summer khakis in a group of dress blues.

At every corner were a pile of slush and a puddle of
black-looking water. For my forty-block trek, I developed a
quickstep-and-broad-jump routine to overcome such ob-
stacles. Snow was coming down hard—about six inches on
the ground—and I had a difficult time seeing where I was
going, so that once in a while I landed in the water or
missed the curb coming up, but my magic Bloomingdale's
galoshes kept me safe. Unlike cross-country skiing, when I
always manage to put on too many clothes and then smother,
walking in this cold was wet and penetrated to my bones,
although the actual temperature was much higher than in
the mountains.

After about ten blocks, I knew that I was going to be late,
so I stopped at a phone booth to call Elaine and tell her. I
said something jocular, like "Send out the Saint Bernards"
if I didn't make it in an hour, knowing full well that if I
didn't make it in an hour and a half, she would probably
come herself to rescue me. As I walked on, I remembered
something that John had written about her before they
were married and just after they had returned to New York
from Hollywood: "She strides along the windy street cutting a swath of light as she goes." What a loving vision of
her that was, and how much he must have loved her.

That was another thing about writing a biography I re-
gretted—there was no way that I could get a sense of that
love, and how it had saved John from despair and useless-
ness, into the book directly. I could only quote a passage or
two from his letters and hope that the point would be

John and Elaine on 17 Mile Drive, Carmel, California, during a break on the *Travels with Charley* trip. Courtesy of Mrs. John Steinbeck.

made. But that wasn't the problem either. The point would be made, but would the reader get a sense of the depth of feeling involved? I doubted it.

I thought of Elaine and how young and strong she seemed. Ten years had gone by, and while I had gotten shorter, fatter, and funnier-looking she had, as far as I could tell, remained the same. So many of the widows I had talked to had been driven to drink in their loneliness, but she never seemed to stop and think about herself. Of all the people I've met over the years, I have never met anyone with less self-pity and more control over her thinking than she has. When we were talking about John's death, she went over the facts calmly, deliberately, and with feeling— but with controlled feeling. Finally, it was I who broke

down—I the listener who had not gone through it broke
down and had to stop and recover before I could hear
any more.

Actually it had been a little more than ten years, and all
during that time I had carefully referred to her husband as
"Steinbeck" or "your husband." I came from a generation
that did not easily call people by their first names. To do
so was an indicator of mutual acceptance, of intimacy—it
marked a distinction that was nice to have and which, like
so many other customs nowadays, is lost forever. I remembered that it was only recently that I was talking to her in
her apartment, asking her, as always, about "her husband."
She stopped me and smiled. "I think it would be all right,"
she said, "if you call him 'John.'"

I had now walked nearly to the apartment building, and
as I stopped for a moment to catch my breath, I looked
down at the trampled snow around me and then up into a
store window of yellow and white and pink and purple
flowers. It was a florist's, and these were spring flowers in
pots for planting. I went in and bought six pots, which they
put in a box lid for me. I walked a half block, and then in by
the fancy-dressed doorman, up in the elevator with the
fancy-dressed elevator man, and down the hall to the door
of the apartment, carrying briefcase and umbrella, dressed
in stocking cap and galoshes, my arms full of spring flowers.

10

The Joys of Being Threatened

Just as soon as the people at Viking set the publication date at July 1, 1983, they began to hedge. I had some sympathy for their situation. Ever since Penguin had taken over, Viking had been in some confusion. There had been some reorganization, and more, apparently, was to come—employees feared for their jobs and wondered if the character of the company would change. At the time my book was supposed to be readied to go to press, the winter of 1982–83, Viking moved its large suite of offices from a Madison Avenue address to one less expensive on the West Side. The move, from all accounts, caused utter chaos for more than a year.

Although I knew that the publishing staff was working under the pressure of several handicaps, I was still impatient with their confusion, and in matters of timing, I had learned not to trust them at all. The publicity department had been in touch with me, and they were interested in having some sort of coming-out party for the book in connection with the annual Steinbeck Festival in Salinas. The festival was attracting visitors from all over the world and was getting an excellent press. It seemed like a perfect opportunity to create a media event, and the publicity staff got in touch with John Gross, director of the Steinbeck Library, and Betty Gheen, president of the Valley Guild, the volunteer charitable organization that owns the Steinbeck house and runs it as a luncheon restaurant and tour attraction.

Between them they arranged to have me present my copy of the manuscript to the library, after which there would be a press reception, and then, on another day, I would give a speech, which would be followed by a reception and book autographing. On a third day, there would be a champagne reception at the Steinbeck House and another autographing. It was of course, as much as anyone could ask for, and I was grateful to John and Betty for endorsing me and the book so heartily. But I began to get hints from Viking that all was not well. "We are going to try out best . . ." sorts of letters began to come. These were followed by "We are not going to be able to publish by the time of the Festival, but we think we can get a couple of hundred books printed and bound and ship them by air to Salinas." My heart was beginning to sink. Knowing how many times my hopes and expectations had been smashed by them in the past, I could smell disaster, even though it was months away.

At about the same time, I got a letter from my agents telling me that they had been informed by the publisher that the book had been "costed out" at a sale price of $43.75. Viking felt that no one would buy the book at that price and asked that I take a cut in royalties, and my agents agreed that I should do so. I tried to put up a fight by asking the agents to see if in return they couldn't get some concessions, perhaps a slightly higher percentage on the paperback royalties. But I didn't even get an acknowledgment of the letter.

In March the galley proofs came out, and I recommended that sets be sent to Sue Riggs and Carlos Baker. Riggs has been the cataloger of the large Steinbeck collection of materials at Stanford and knew a great deal about Steinbeck, as well as having worked in the past as an editor. Baker, of course, was the Hemingway biographer, but not only did he know about biography, he had written several pieces about Steinbeck and was a precise and very scrupulous writer. Between them most of the errors neglected by the copy editors were put to rights, and my wife and I made our contribution, one of us reading the manuscript aloud and the other checking the proofs. This was hard going for me because I had read through the manuscript so many times that I saw words that were no longer there.

By early May my wife and I were beginning to make arrangements for the summer, looking forward to the first really carefree vacation in years. We had a feeling that everything was pretty well on track and that the book really would come out. But our growing sanguinity was blasted by a phone call. I was told that there was some possibility that I might be sued. The Steinbeck estate, my agents (who were also agents for the estate), and Viking had conferred and decided that the book had passages that might offend certain members of the Steinbeck family (namely, the two sons). The manuscript would have to be gone over by lawyers for the agency and for the publisher. Changes would probably have to be made.

My first reaction was a feeling that my foreboding about the summer's activities to promote the book had come true: publication would be delayed for months, and there would be no books at Salinas. My second reaction was some wonder at what had happened to cause this sudden concern. If there were legal questions, why hadn't they been answered long before this? I was as certain as I could be that there was nothing libelous in the manuscript, for I had been conscious of this as a problem while writing and had been very careful. My editor, Bill Strachan, had expressed to me a similar reaction—there was nothing that had seemed libelous or even objectionable. But more than this, I knew that I had gone out of my way to be fair—probably too far. If the sons were going to make a fuss, I didn't see on what basis they were going to do so.

I knew, however, that if you are going to give a manuscript to a bunch of lawyers, in this case, two bunches of lawyers, they are going to earn their pay. In their ultraconservative way, there was no chance that they wouldn't come up with items that posed some risk. And, of course, my problem would be that they would have no motive whatsoever to take any risks at all—they were paid to protect the estate and the agency on the one side and the publisher on the other. I also knew that there was fear in New York and that the atmosphere for trying to defend freedom of speech couldn't have been worse.

Lillian Hellman was suing Mary McCarthy for saying on the Dick Cavett TV show that Hellman's memoirs were full of lies. I didn't have much love for Mary McCarthy, for on the same show, in her waspish way, she declared that John Steinbeck was the most overrated author in recent American literary history. But she was alone in this battle and not a wealthy woman, and nearly everyone connected with literature and publishing, I included, felt a little sorry for her. What she said, probably in hyperbole, was relatively mild in the context of the normal course of critical debate. Hellman could have gotten on Cavett's or someone else's TV show and refuted the charges and counterattacked or written a nasty column for the *New York Review of Books* or taken any number of other avenues of reply open to someone of her stature. That she should reply by suing was unsettling, to say the least, because, under the law, even if McCarthy should defend herself successfully, she would have to pay her own costs.

Concern about my book, if not generated by the Hellman-McCarthy battle, was certainly heightened by it. I could feel it in the semihysteria of the phone calls and letters I was receiving. So, even though I was sure I had nothing to worry about, I began to worry. It seemed more and more certain with every passing week that the book either was going to be badly crippled or would not be published at all. I had to muster the courage to face the possibility that, even though no one had actually threatened legal action, the book might very well go down the drain simply out of fear.

It took weeks for the lawyers to go over the manuscript, weeks that under the pressure of fear and dread seemed to stretch out endlessly. To the lawyers, this was just another routine review, but to me, it was a very large portion of my life. At last in late June, I received a letter reporting some two-dozen items that had been noted by the lawyers as requiring change. This doesn't sound like much, but the space devoted to the sons in the biography was relatively small to begin with, which meant that almost every reference to them in the book that had any negative connotations at all had to be modified. Almost all of the changes were, to my mind, outrageous. All young boys misbehave, and all young boys have some conflict with their fathers—not to mention the circumstances that children of famous people have their problems and the children of a bitter divorce do too. You would have to see the changes in the manuscript, which for obvious reasons I cannot cite here, to realize in what bad shape the First Amendment is in. We think we have freedom of speech if we do not unjustly besmirch someone's reputation, but don't you believe it.

What was infuriating was, first, that no demands for change had been made: all of this was in *anticipation* of possible objections. And, second, there was not a damned thing I could do. Normally the writer's agent would stand up for his point of view and even hire a lawyer, if such a champion was needed. But my agents, representing also the estate, were more fearful of suit than enamored of the book. They felt that by protecting themselves they were also acting in my interest and protecting me. I felt that the agency, McIntosh and Otis, was honest and well intentioned (although I often was made to feel like a poor cousin in my dealings with them), but there was bound to be, from my point of view, some conflict of interest. I thought that I might have made a mistake in accepting Elizabeth Otis's offer to represent me. She was gone now, and none of the people at the agency knew me personally.

Eventually, lawyers for the two sons (or, as they were always euphemistically referred to, "the two boys"—who were in their late thirties) got into the act, and there were, at this point, further objections. So we had three sets of lawyers, for the estate, the agents, and the publisher, all eager to make changes and no one on the other side with any clout willing to say, "Now, just a minute." I felt alone, standing on a battlefield holding up some kind of tattered banner, while everyone else had ducked for cover.

And, indeed, I was alone during the "negotiations," as they might be called, since I was in the mountains working, while my wife had returned to her teaching job in San Diego. There weren't any negotiations, really. The process went on over the phone to New York just about every day for several weeks. Bill Strachan would call, and he would read a passage objected to. Then he would suggest a possible alternative. The change would knock all sense out of the passage or, occasionally, take away the main point of the whole section. I would be so angry I couldn't talk. So I would fume and fuss and kick rocks for twenty-four hours and the next day face the fact that I had no choice. A couple of times I said, "No—screw the book and the whole thing. I will not change that. . . . I don't care what happens." Bill would say, "I don't blame you. It is a silly change that really makes hash of the whole page." Patiently he would call back the next day and explain what I already knew: if I didn't make the change, then I would not get the necessary permissions. Without permissions, no book.

Each time I was forced to this point, I felt something like I am sure a woman feels when she has been raped. I felt I was losing my integrity, and the book was losing its truth and meaning, bit by bit. Part of my emotional breakdown at the time was due to the fact that I really had no one on my side to talk to. I needed advice and, if not sympathy, at least an objective point of view in regard to what was happening. In desperation, I called everyone I knew in New York not connected with the Steinbecks or McIntosh and Otis, in an effort to find a lawyer that specialized in publication law. I called and called for two days, but I couldn't get a name. I really didn't have the money for a lawyer, but I was more than ready to borrow it.

It may be that I was taking the whole thing too hard. Later, when I talked to a newspaperwoman of my acquaintance, she expressed the view that what I had gone through was to be expected. She had her stories reviewed and "editorially censored" all the time, and I was being supersensitive. Perhaps. But even now, years later, I don't feel about the book as I once did. Compliments on it restored some of its luster for me, but I am still not sure whether or not I should have taken a stand. It might have been better for my peace of mind and the soundness of my soul if like Bartleby I had had the courage to simply say, "I prefer not to."

I may have reacted too strongly, but I am convinced that everyone else overreacted in the other direction, unwilling to take any risks, such as they might have been, at all. Some evidence of this came later. While covering the Salinas Steinbeck Festival, a reporter from the *New York Times* got wind of the controversy I had just gone through. He talked to me (I had been asked not to comment very specifically on what had happened, and so I was rather vague), to Bill Strachan and others at Viking, to people at the festival, and to representatives of the estate. In a half-page article, headlined "Family Members' Objections Delay Publication of Steinbeck Biography," the reporter traced the controversy and then pointed to one of the key items that had been censored: in the original manuscript, "[Steinbeck] is portrayed as having been hopelessly in love with her [Gwyn, John's second wife], but that, especially toward the end of their relationship, she cared little for him, and when she finally left him, she claimed—perhaps falsely—that one of their sons was not his."

How the reporter had got this information I don't know—the ways of the *New York Times* are mysterious. A few bound galleys had been sent out to reviewers before the whole process of publication had ground to a halt, and it may be that he somehow located one of these and then, somehow, made a comparison—but that doesn't explain how he knew where to look. At any rate, this was one of the key points of argument between me and the lawyers. I had felt that this was the lowest point in John's life, an extremely dramatic moment, and that the whole structure of the book as a story would be weakened by taking out this detail.

I didn't know the fine points of the law, but common sense told me that it would be impossible for me to be successfully sued for reporting a lie, as a lie, told by a dead person. This was the straw that broke my back. I went out into the woods and thought about my position for several hours. I was so agitated that I called Carlos Baker (whom I had corresponded with on a few occasions but had never met). He advised that my problems were not unusual and that if I had something to say that the lawyers wouldn't let me say, I should put it in an article and publish it later. But the only way I could continue was on the basis that it was no longer my book, and I really didn't want to have anything more to do with it.

Now, however, here were the words which had been the cause of our great debate and all of my agitation and soul searching, spread across the pages of the country's leading newspaper and from there syndicated and reprinted in newspapers all over the country. There were so many ironies in this that I couldn't keep track of them all.

I remembered the occasion several years earlier when the information had been given to me. I had gone to New York on one of my last trips before I began work on the manuscript. At this point Elizabeth Otis had retired, after holding on to control of the agency long after retirement age, and reluctantly had passed on the management to an associate, Shirley Fisher. Both of them had been very close to John, and I had come to know them fairly well over a period of a decade. I stopped by the office to say hello to Shirley, and she invited me to lunch. We talked about my progress and plans for the manuscript, and Shirley, as always, talked at length about John. We had several drinks over a period of two hours or so, and things were getting a bit confused when Shirley excused herself to make a phone call. She came back to say that she had set up a meeting and that I should come to Elizabeth's apartment that afternoon at four.

I hadn't the slightest idea what was going on, but I had noticed that Shirley had been thoughtful and distracted, and apparently this was to be some kind of conference. When I arrived and was shown into the living room by the maid, I noted not only that Shirley already was there, with Elizabeth, but that Mavis McIntosh was there also. This was a surprise. Mavis had started the literary agency with Elizabeth but after a decade had left the company owing to a protracted illness. Later she had gone into partnership with someone else to form a new agency. I knew that she had remained friendly with Elizabeth, but I also knew that they had not been in close touch for many years. Her presence seemed to signify that something very special was in the air.

Elizabeth's living room was always dark, the blinds partly down behind heavy draperies. The room was furnished very formally, in velvets and brocades and dark mahogany woods, chairs and sofas arranged in a square around the room and in front of them coffee tables with silver candy bowls and cut-glass ashtrays and cigarette boxes. Here and there a lighted table lamp barely made yellow progress against the gloom. Next to me, on one side of the room, a thin, almost tiny woman, sitting stiffly upright in a straight-backed chair, was Elizabeth. To my left, on the adjoining side of the room, Shirley sat, then stood, then sat again, agitated and impatient. Across from Elizabeth and me was Mavis, who, dressed in a dark business suit with a red rose in her lapel, sat calmly, waiting. And then to our right was Chase Horton, former bookstore owner and long-time friend of Elizabeth. We sat in formation, and the atmosphere was a combination of board meeting and seance.

Shirley had had more to drink since I left her. Passionate even in her most sober moments, she was now almost hysterical. "For God's sake, you've got to tell him. Now. There may not be another chance," she was saying to Elizabeth.

.

Elizabeth Otis (left) and Elaine after the Viking Press news conference announcing John's Nobel Prize, 1962. Courtesy of the Bracken Library, Ball State University Library, Muncie, Indiana.

Elizabeth was sitting very still, her face composed into a stiff mask, her hands folded in her lap. John had been her pride and joy. She had promoted him, advised him, nagged at him, stood by him. When he was alive, she protected him from the press, from the public, from the pressures of fame. After his death, she did everything she could to protect his reputation and promote the welfare of his work. She was grudging in the permissions she gave to reprint his work, and she was antagonistic toward anyone that she suspected might not have John's best interests at heart. It had taken me a long time to win her confidence, but as far as John was concerned, I don't think she ever totally trusted anybody.

Elizabeth remained still, and the silence became strained. Chase, who was getting along in years, felt the strain but seemed to miss the import of the occasion. He began to ask me about the book and then launched into a story about John riding the Long Island train into town. No one was listening except me.

When Chase finished, again there was silence. Shirley got up and began to pace in front of her chair. "He's the *official* biographer, Elizabeth," Shirley declared, and repeated, "He's the official biographer." She stood in front of both of us, short and heavyset, peering at Elizabeth through her glasses. Her voice broke a bit as she said, "For God's sake, Elizabeth, you have got to tell him. He has to know."

Elizabeth looked up at Shirley and said, "What is it you want me to say? I really don't know what you want me to say, Shirley." Shirley shook her head and sat down. She was crying and took off her glasses to wipe them with a handkerchief. Mavis sat looking at the walls and ceiling and said nothing.

Shirley said, "You know very well what I'm talking about. You've got to tell him about Gwyn."

There was silence again for a moment as Elizabeth seemed to draw herself together. When she spoke, she didn't look at me but stared straight forward, out toward the center of the room. In a thin voice, weary and old, she seemed to measure every word as she said, "During the war—when John was overseas getting shot at—Gwyn wrote to him. She taunted him with her affairs. Tried to hurt him as much as possible. She never loved him—just used him. When he left to be a correspondent, she took it as an insult and tried in every way possible to get back at him. She was insane. John should never have married her. She never told the truth in her life."

When she stopped, Mavis spoke up, which startled me for a moment: "When she and Carol were fighting over John, both of them claimed to be pregnant. Of course, both of them were lying."

Shirley looked at Elizabeth and said, "Go on. Tell him the whole thing."

Elizabeth coughed and covered her mouth with a small handkerchief. She had been ill for some time. She turned to me: "When Gwyn told John that she was going to divorce him, she was still trying to hurt him, to get even for all the wrongs he had done her—all in her head. She told him that Johnny wasn't his—that someone else was his father. Of course, she made it up . . . made it up, all of it."

Shirley looked at me. She was still crying. "Can you imagine how he felt? Do you have any idea how much she hurt him?" she said. "Can you imagine how poor Johnny felt?"

Of course, the festival was for me a disaster. What I had looked forward to as my moment of triumph had turned to ashes, black as my file folders that had dissolved in acid near the beginning of my work on the book. I had a mental picture of the two sons laughing, laughing, laughing at all the chaos they had caused and enjoying my discomfiture enormously. It was embarrassing. At every gathering I had to make excuses for the book that should have been there but wasn't, answer questions, and try to put the best face possible on a celebration that no longer had any purpose. I was swallowing antacid tablets at an enormous rate. My stomach churned in nervous exhaustion, and my head throbbed with hatred. If I didn't take myself in hand, I was going to end up a basket case, caused not by those who had wished me harm but by my own self-pity.

What helped turn me around was a wild man by the name of Gordon Joblon. In his late fifties, he had been on top of the world, an executive vice-president of Shearson in New York City and a TV commentator on investments. Then he had a massive heart attack. He dropped everything and moved to Salinas and into retirement. Expecting the worst, he bought a house only a couple of blocks from the hospital. But after only a few months of enforced idleness, he couldn't stand it any more and began to work for various volunteer organizations, including Friends of the John Steinbeck Library, an organization that had lain somewhat dormant until he energized it by becoming its president.

He spent much of his time at the library, manning a table near the entrance, where he sold copies of John's books, posters, and "I Love John Steinbeck" T-shirts. These activities were part of a plan to raise money to purchase the manuscript of *The Pearl* for the library. When people came to the festival or at other times during the year to the library on a Steinbeck pilgrimage, they were inevitably greeted first by Joblon at his table, where, while pushing T-shirts, he would answer questions about Steinbeck points of interest in the Salinas-Monterey area and about Steinbeck's fiction. He had prepared himself for these questions by reading all of John's works and most of the criticism and by talking to me and to Pauline Pearson, the library's historian. He had also run into a number of the locals who had known John or about him, so that, in addition to answering questions, he had developed a repertoire of Steinbeck stories. One of the most peculiar problems he had was that visitors, perhaps because of his beard, sometimes mistook him for Steinbeck. In the weeks just before the festival, six adults and two children approached him as Steinbeck and asked questions. Why any adult would think that a writer would be sitting in the lobby of a library named after him waiting to answer questions I don't know.

Joblon was at his best when he was talking to the many reporters who were sent to the festival from papers all over the world. He gave them the tour of the library and the deluxe spiel, including not only stories about John in Salinas and a description of the activities and goals of the Friends but also a boost for the Steinbeck Foundation, which had plans to build a special wing onto the library, providing more room for display of materials. Article after article written about the festival turned out to be more Joblon than anything else.

In preparation for my arrival that summer, Gordon had gone to the local Cadillac dealer and told him that a very special VIP was coming and that, for the sake of Salinas's reputation and standing in the world, the VIP should have a new Cadillac to drive during his stay at the festival. So when my wife and I arrived at the San Jose airport, we were picked up by Gordon in "our" new car. Use of the car was very flattering, but also worrisome and, for us, difficult. Neither my wife nor I had ever driven anything larger or more luxurious than our VW bus and a little Opel. That evening, when we were supposed to meet the Joblons for dinner, we sat in our Cadillac, completely intimidated by the instruments and options, wondering how to turn on the headlights. Although I even got out of the car and knelt on the floormat, peering everywhere, I couldn't find a switch. At last we determined to start off, at dusk, without them. As we left the curb, the lights came on by themselves, which was rather frightening—what else would the car decide to do by itself that we didn't know about?

My down-in-the-dumps attitude was completely foreign to Gordon's approach to life. The controversy that I had hated was to him a godsend. "The more controversy, the better," he declared, after I had given him an abbreviated version of my sad story. "It'll help sell more books." We were sitting in his living room having wine and cheese before going on to dinner. Joblon looked more like a college professor than I did, with his silver-rimmed glasses, gray hair combed straight back, and closely trimmed gray beard—certainly more like a professor than a successful stockbroker. Like most other bright people, he loved puns—the more farfetched, the better. He had been working on the titles of John's books and tried out a few of his most recent on us: "Steinbeck's Knitting Guide—*The Purl*," "A Jewish Seeker—*The Gropes of Roth*," "The Missing Letter—*The 'C' of Ortes*." My wife groaned repeatedly, with genuine feeling, and I told him that they were the very worst puns I had ever heard, and he was delighted.

Since along with his other achievements Gordon was also a colonel in the army reserve, he and his wife were taking us to dinner at the officers' club at nearby Fort Ord. We left the Cadillac and got into his big Lincoln, and he chauffeured us to the fort, in through the back way. As we drove by the various bivouac areas and instructional ranges, I thought of my own time at Fort Ord and how, as a lowly corporal, I never would have dreamed that I would sometime come to the officers' club in a Lincoln driven by a colonel. The scene in the club was like a Technicolor movie of the British raj in India. The large, beautifully decorated dining room with its gleaming silver and crystal and white linen tablecloths was many worlds away from the mess halls that I suddenly recalled with a shudder for the first time in years. I remembered getting up at 3:00 A.M. to go on KP, peeling potatoes, like the sad sacks in a Mauldin cartoon, and then washing up, including cleaning the garbage cans and the grease traps under the large galvanized sinks. I almost lost my appetite.

The prime rib we were served was nothing like the liver with the consistency of shoe leather we inevitably had for dinner during my tenure as an enlisted man. Our mess sergeant was arrested for selling most of his rations of beef to restaurants in town. We could have told the MPs months earlier that something was wrong. But even after the cook's arrest, the food didn't improve—an intractability which is a pretty good definition of the army.

During the days that followed, I found myself cheering Gordon on, as he tried to stir up the controversy over the book and give it as much drama as possible. Maybe he was right; maybe it was good for the book, and maybe "the boys" were cooking their own goose. He spent quite a long time, he reported proudly to me later, giving the whole story to a reporter for the *New York Times*. At the same time, he and John Gross, the library's director, had worked out a scheme whereby those who wanted to buy a copy of the book could fill out a form, pay their money, and then receive an autographed copy later in the mail. I gave my speech at the library to a packed house and the following day gave another short talk to those assembled at the Steinbeck House reception. Mrs. Ainsworth, almost ninety years old, was there, having made a great effort to come over from Pacific Grove to see me and offer her congratulations. Of course, she hadn't seen the size of the book yet.

When it came time for us to return to San Diego, Gordon and his wife, Delores, offered to drive us to the airport in the Cadillac. We left early, allowing an hour and half beyond the time we figured it would take to get there. The highway was busy, but we had no trouble until we got to Gilroy. At that point we ran into a traffic jam that slowed us to a stop-and-go crawl. We had encountered the crowd returning from the Gilroy Garlic Festival. Salinas had Steinbeck; Gilroy had garlic. And the garlic was the clear winner, attracting, with such delicacies as garlic ice cream, tens of thousands of visitors a day.

After nearly an hour of slow movement, we began to worry that we might miss our plane. At the turnoff to the airport, we made a dash down the suddenly clear road, making desperate plans for a last-minute rush onto the airplane. I would grab the luggage out of the trunk, while my wife, Sue, and Gordon would run in with the tickets and try to save our places. To speed things up, Gordon thought that he should release the trunk lock. On his Lincoln he could push a lever in the glove box, and, sure enough, there was a similar switch in the Cadillac. As we made our final approach to the terminal, with cabs and buses on either side pulling in and out from the curb, Gordon pushed the button. Instead of just unlatching, the trunk lid popped all the way up. It looked as though we had just fired a missile, and in his shock Gordon swerved, almost hitting a cab. The huge lid blocked all view of the rear and made it almost impossible to pull over to the right and park. Gordon's wife, Delores, leaned out the window, yelling and waving warnings while Gordon screeched to a halt in a no-parking zone. Like the sudden scattering of Keystone Kops, I jumped out to get the luggage while simultaneously Gordon and Sue stormed the terminal.

I had just made the door when I saw Gordon, who in a burst of speed had outdistanced my wife, yelling and gesturing to the guards at the security check. He was telling

the guards and everyone standing in line that some important people were about to miss their plane and did they
mind if he rushed us right through. The crowd stared at us
in puzzlement, since neither Sue nor I looked like a rock
star or a baseball player. On the other side of the metal de-
tector, Gordon grabbed one of the suitcases from me and
led the way as the three of us ran down the corridor to the
departure gate. Sue and I were on the plane and in the air
before we realized that here was a man who not too long
ago had had a heart attack. We were in dread of the possible consequences until we could get to a phone upon
landing and assure ourselves that Gordon Joblon had survived. Not only had he survived, but he had, he informed
us, just returned the Cadillac to the dealer without a scratch.
"What about 'The Vicars'?" he asked.
"'The Vicars,'" I said. "I don't know—what are you talking about?"
He paused dramatically: "The Pastors of Heaven!"
I groaned.

During this period of worry about lawsuits and the Steinbeck Festival, I had been called on the phone several times
by a Tom Wills (as I will call him), who introduced himself
as a reviewer for the *Christian Science Monitor*. The *Monitor* had a special place in my life. My mother had become a
Christian Science practitioner and teacher who wrote articles for the church's religious publications. My uncle had
been the Washington, D.C., news bureau chief for the
Monitor for years, and Dick Allman, who had taken many
of the landscape photos for the Steinbeck biography, had
been the West Coast photographer for the *Monitor*. Although I was not religious, and no doubt a disappointment
to my mother, many of our family and family friends were,
and a number of close friends from childhood, shared by
Dick and me, were Christian Scientists.
    So when Wills called, I tended to feel that it was a mem-
ber of the "family" calling, and although I didn't believe
that a rave or even totally positive review was in any way

guaranteed, I did feel confident that the *Monitor,* because
of its reputation for fairness and thoroughness, would give
the book every chance. This open-mindedness was important, because I knew even then, before any reviews had appeared, that some periodicals and critics held Steinbeck
in such contempt that any biography, no matter what its
merits, would be condemned out of hand as a waste of
paper, especially if it didn't spend most of its space de-
nigrating the author. Since I had written a book that neither uncritically praised Steinbeck nor raked him over the
coals, I knew that I was going to take a beating from a number of major periodicals.

Although Wills called often and usually during the hour
when we were fixing dinner (and if it is my turn to cook, I
am always in a frenzy trying to get everything to come out
at the same time), and although he admitted not yet having
had time to read the book, I felt bound to do everything I
could to cooperate. At the same time, of course, I was talking to several people who were reviewers or book editors
for other periodicals, so that my conversations with Wills
were not unusual except for their frequency. He began calling me during the time that I was alone in the mountains,
battling day by day my conscience and the demands of the
lawyers. His was a friendly voice, and I found it a relief to
talk to him, confiding in him my ongoing troubles, without
going into any detail about specific arguments.

It became clear after a time, however, that he was not
regularly employed by the *Monitor* but was a free-lance
journalist who had other things in mind besides just doing a
review of the book. It also became clear to me that he knew
very little about Steinbeck and almost nothing about the
criticism and biography that had already been written.
Why he had been selected by the newspaper to do the review I couldn't imagine, except that he lived in the Monterey area. Our conversations became more frequent after
the exposé of the threatened lawsuits in the *New York
Times,* and he indicated to me that he had lined up another
article possibility with the *San Francisco Chronicle* Sunday

magazine. Following on the *Times* article, he went on to interview Thom Steinbeck, who as it turned out was living temporarily in Monterey.

In the meantime, the changes in the manuscript had been completed, and several weeks later the lawyer for the two Steinbeck sons indicated informally that, since we had met all of their objections, they had no plans to sue. It was not a particularly reassuring message but did relieve some, if not all, of the pressure. However, it was not long after that I got word of new threats. Sometime after meeting with Thom at an event called the Cannery Row Festival— which may have been only a coincidence—William Brown, the former Carol Steinbeck's second husband, and Ed Ricketts, Jr., indicated their dissatisfaction with the book and possible intention to sue the author and the publisher. This came as something as a shock, since I thought I had been on good terms with both men. It also was strange, since both appeared to be acting in "defense" of dead relatives who had been treated fairly, for the most part favorably, and at great length. What was even stranger was that the book was not yet published, and I had to wonder, Where did they get a copy of the galleys? From the ubiquitous Thom Steinbeck?

I also wondered what it was in people—or in the Constitution and law of the land, for that matter—that led them to think that if a book didn't meet their expectations they were justified in collecting money from the book's author. The thought came to me that perhaps they had no intention of following through (although I did get a threatening letter from Brown's lawyers) but had just gotten together over a few drinks with Thom and had decided it would serve that arrogant academic (me) right if they served him up a little pain and anguish.

Down in the dumpster once again, I told Tom Wills the next time he called that it appeared to me that others were being encouraged to sue. Wills followed this as his lead and was soon interviewing both Bill Brown and Ed Ricketts's son. For all of his professed sympathy, I seemed to detect a bit of sadism in Wills's calls as he pointedly aimed Brown's and Ricketts's charges at me, to see, I was sure, how I would react.

Indeed, within the controversy and my renewed low spirits, he had developed the idea for his *San Francisco Chronicle* article. He had been in touch with a group of older men who had found a "new" Steinbeck house in Pacific Grove, and he called me up to ask me if I would mind, the next time I was in northern California, going over to that house and meeting him there. Wills thought it would make a good article if I, who had been suffering the slings and arrows of threatened economic disaster, would tell him further of my problems in a setting where, it might be reasonably assumed, Steinbeck himself had sat and brooded over rejected manuscripts and money problems. It seemed to me to be a rather contrived piece of journalism, but, desperate for sympathy, I agreed.

When I arrived at the house, I saw for the first time the man whose deep voice I had heard so many times over the phone. He was tall and very thin, with thick glasses and a pointed beard. He wore a European sailor's cap scrunched down over his head, and a wool muffler covered his throat above a tweed sport jacket. He smoked constantly and had a racking cough—indeed, as I looked at him, I thought of the tubercular, starving art student that one might have found in Paris at the turn of the century.

I learned that Wills really didn't know these men much better than I did. The atmosphere was very strange. I was reminded of a Browning Society or Theosophical Society meeting where the older members were graciously ushering two new, younger members into the inner sanctum. The owner of the house and his two friends were dedicated to a cause, that of giving this house its due, and their manner was hushed, almost religious, in extolling the importance and virtues of their "shrine." While they were showing me a deed to the house, which showed John co-owner with his sisters (they must have been left the house jointly in their father's will), Wills was trying to get me to repeat to him, in this setting for the purposes of his article, some of the lamentations I had already visited upon him over the phone.

The three men were very sincere and dedicated and wanted desperately to present their case to us; Wills was very intense in taking notes, but, with a bad cold, he had to stop every few minutes and blow his nose; and the more I dwelt on the injustices of my life, the more I felt like crying. The whole scene was so absurd that by the end of the interview I was in fairly good spirits. One of the older men, with great kindness, told me, as I was leaving, that I shouldn't worry—Wills was not only a writer but a man with the soul of a poet and that he would bring justice to my cause, if anyone could. As we parted, we shook hands all around.

11

Pride and Prejudice

As fall approached, I learned that the publication date had been reset for January 16, 1984, which seemed to me, like the July date, a very peculiar choice. Why not in time for Christmas, or, if not that, the following spring? I began my teaching routine, and at home I began cleaning up the mess in my office. I emptied my filing cabinets, sorted out the contents, and boxed what I thought should be saved. Over the years, items had been put back in the wrong folders, and folders had been put into the wrong categories. I took a rag and washed my desk and then waxed it. I cleaned my typewriter. I filled a bucket with soapy water and scrubbed down the walls in an effort to remove the yellow stains from my pipe smoke. I reshelved my books and put them all back in order. I took my miscellaneous drawer—the thin middle drawer of my oak desk (a desk my mother bought for me that I used when I was a child)—and reorganized it, fitting in dividers and trays to hold all my odds and ends accumulated ever since the San Francisco International Exposition of 1939. And when I was through, I was thoroughly depressed by the neatness of it all.

I looked at a desk that for the first time in over a decade was polished and nearly empty. I looked at a typewriter that no longer had dark edges and grimy keys from my grubby hands. And I wondered, What was I going to do now?

It would be hard for me to go back to literary criticism. All the things that I had complained about I now missed— no more travel, no more interviews and meeting new people, no more sudden discoveries. And the excitement of the mail—no more letters to look forward to. When the mailman came now was to me largely a matter of indifference. But also I had come to dislike criticism. What I had been doing, I felt, was building something, creating something, and what criticism did so often was to tear things down—to mock, disparage, and belittle. That wasn't the whole truth, of course, but somehow being a biographer seemed a nobler calling.

My negative feelings about criticism had grown largely in response to reading all the criticism that Steinbeck had received during his lifetime. My own position was that he had written one masterpiece (*The Grapes of Wrath*), several other exceptional works that would be read for some time into the future (*In Dubious Battle*, *Of Mice and Men*, *The Long Valley*, *The Log from the "Sea of Cortez*," *Cannery Row*, and *The Pearl*), some books that weren't memorable (*To a God Unknown*, *The Wayward Bus*, *Sweet Thursday*, and *The Winter of Our Discontent*), a few very bad books (*Cup of Gold*, *The Moon Is Down*, *Burning Bright*, and *The Short Reign of Pippin IV*), and a book I couldn't make up my mind about, *East of Eden*. By no stretch of the imagination did I think everything he had written was lasting and important, nor did I feel I had some personal stake in defending the merits of any particular work. So it didn't bother me to see reviews of his books that were negative; even when I disagreed, I found some very negative reviews quite perceptive. There are matters that informed readers can argue about, and I took that as a matter of course.

What bothered me was when a periodical, such as *Time*, apparently took an editorial stand against Steinbeck, never giving his work a fair shake. Or when particular critics expressed a prejudice against all things western, against a writer who had such a deep sense of the ecological interrelatedness of man and nature—implying that such a sensibility was nonsense, of no importance, or held by the author only superficially. But what upset me most was the discovery of how much of the criticism of Steinbeck's work was just gratuitously nasty. We have an unfortunate tendency to take at their word critics whose primary drive in life is to demonstrate their own superiority. They cannot read, because their ego gets in the way of any outside reception—with the ability to empathize or to take a different perspective.

Steinbeck had more than his share of good reviews throughout his career, and several important critics were favorably inclined toward his work—although certainly not praising everything—but he always had problems with what we call the eastern literary establishment. There were several reasons for this: he was a westerner; he was a very popular writer; he had a sense of humor and wrote several comedies and farces; he tried to stretch himself and refused to write the same book over and over again; he wrote no criticism himself or serious literary essays; and although he was an intellectual, in nearly every sense of the word, he refused to play the role and wear the badges. He remained always the outsider, the individualist.

But perhaps the most powerful and invidious reason he has become the most controversial—in terms of reputation—of all modern American novelists has been his politics, or lack of them. Throughout his life he was squeezed on one side by the conservative scorn of the popular press—Hearst, Chandler, and Luce—and on the other by the snobbish disdain of the liberal intellectual journals, particularly the *New Republic* and the *New York Times Book Review*. The potent emotionalism inherent in the political approach to literary criticism can be seen in reviews of Steinbeck's work from nearly the beginning of his career to the end. Often negative reviews of his novels are not disagreements or criticism of artistic weaknesses as much as they are attacks involving personal disparagement. In 1936, while reviewing *In Dubious Battle* for the *Nation*, Mary McCarthy did not just express dislike for the novel and disagreement with Steinbeck's approach and ideas; she felt compelled to express contempt for the novel and its author—what he has to say is "childish"; his verbalizations are "infantile."

McCarthy's nastiness brings to the fore another peculiar aspect of Steinbeck criticism: wrapped up in their own political emotions, reviewers on the right or the left seldom paid much attention to what Steinbeck was actually saying. From the beginning of his career to the end they were, instead, telling him what he should be saying. McCarthy, totally involved in her own ideas, does not understand what Steinbeck has written in *In Dubious Battle*, nor, apparently, does she have any interest in attempting to find out. Like many of the most prominent critics and reviewers of the 1930s, McCarthy is a Marxist. She is irritated by Steinbeck's failure to write a Marxist tract. In her view, anything else, in dealing with the "labor struggle," is either irrelevant or silly.

The novels that caused the most political furor, *In Dubious Battle* and *The Grapes of Wrath*, were written relatively early in Steinbeck's career, yet the labels attached to him followed him for the rest of his life. For over thirty years, as I have said, *Time* expressed its antagonism for him as a "proletarian" writer (taking just the opposite position from Mary McCarthy's). It is hard to imagine the depth of hatred for Steinbeck held by someone on that magazine, presumably Henry Luce, which would feed on itself and fester for so long. On the other hand, the Marxists who tended to applaud his early writing and who tried to use Steinbeck for their own purposes in whatever ways they could, scolded him when he turned away from the subject of farm labor. I think one has to wonder, in retrospect, how much of Steinbeck's alleged decline in quality (now the standard academic judgment) following *The Grapes of Wrath* asserted by critics was real and how much simply the expression of disinterest in Steinbeck's new subjects by Marxists who were disappointed that he did not write *The Grapes of Wrath* over and over again.

The image of Steinbeck as former Marxist was carried on

John at an onion farm on the Mekong River, in northeast Thailand, 1967.
Courtesy of Mrs. John Steinbeck.

and on by both the right, which never forgave him, and the
left, which held up his years of glory, the *Grapes* years, as
constant reproach to his degeneracy. Liberal-radical attacks
on Steinbeck in his late years were particularly acri-
monious. During the early years of the Vietnam War he
was only one of many writers and correspondents who
tended to have hawkish views. Yet the bitterest commen-
tary was reserved for Steinbeck—the Marxists were particularly upset with him for acting what was, in their minds,
the traitor. They had the gall first to make him a Marxist,
which he never was, and then to accuse him of betraying
that which they had made him out to be. Peter Collier, for
example, in *Ramparts*, compares him to Ezra Pound during World War II and thus presumably to Pound's fascism

and giving of aid and comfort to the enemy, a very peculiar parallel when one considers that Steinbeck's "crime" was support for American troops fighting under difficult circumstances in a foreign war.

The Marxists advocated a long view of history; what they did not like was that Steinbeck, as an ecologist, took an even longer view. What Mary McCarthy was objecting to, of course, was Steinbeck's *use* of the labor struggle, which has ultimate importance to her, to make other points. As time went by and Steinbeck's subjects shifted to other aspects of human experience, the two things he was most often criticized for, particularly by Marxist and liberal critics, was his philosophy and his use of allegory.

Normally, that a fiction writer has a philosophy of any substance or that his work has the depth of several interpretative levels should be cause for congratulations. However, to left-leaning critics such as Edmund Wilson and Alfred Kazin, Steinbeck's philosophy is not even worth bothering with (nor, according to these critics, is the California experience rich enough to support any sort of "class A" literature), and his use of allegory is seen as a fault. It is one thing to examine a novelist's philosophy in all its aspects and applications and then disagree with it or refute it and quite another simply to call it a "pseudo-philosophy" or, as does Kazin, dismiss it as vague "biologism."

Steinbeck's usual practice of developing several levels of meaning is often referred to by these critics as "fuzzy-mindedness," which somehow suggests that the author is moonlighting and not paying enough attention to his main job. What Wilson, Kazin, Arthur Mizener, and others wanted Steinbeck to do was to stay in the Long Valley and write about poor people. What they valued in Steinbeck's work was the realistic surface of a few relatively early novels which from their point of view dealt with "important things." Once the novelist's surface realism shifts to other subjects, they have no use for him whatsoever. But not only do they dislike what he is doing, they hate him for it. Indeed, by the time of the Nobel Prize, it had become de rigueur in order to certify one's intellectual credentials to show as much contempt for Steinbeck as possible.

To cite just one example among many, Stanley Edgar Hyman wrote that he began to lose interest in Steinbeck after the shift in "social commitment" marked by *Of Mice and Men* as opposed to *The Moon Is Down*. That shift away from commitment seemed to him confirmed by *Cannery Row*, which he found "merely an insipid watering-down of Steinbeck's engaging earlier book *Tortilla Flat*." "I stopped reading him," he adds. Later, however, he was sent *The Winter of Our Discontent* for review but decided that it was "far too trivial and dishonest a book to waste space on." When Hyman learns of the Nobel Prize, given in response to Steinbeck's recent publication of *Winter*, he finds the choice and its occasion incredible. He rereads the book and finds it confirms his earlier impression of it. "It is the purest soap opera, a work of almost inconceivable badness." When he discovers on the dust jacket that the book had been praised by Lewis Gannet and Saul Bellow, Hyman decides that "to assume their honesty I must disparage their intelligence."

For all his experience with and examination of mass movements and political radicalism, Steinbeck could never really comprehend the motives for such intense acrimony. In his letters he questions why a novel, even if it is not a very good novel, should evoke so much hatred. And while he did not comment publicly very often on the criticism of his work—showing for the most part an admirable restraint in the face of enormous provocation—he did go on public record, saying:

It is interesting to me that so many critics, instead of making observations, are led to bring charges. It is not observed that I find it valid to understand man as an animal before I am prepared to know him as man. It is charged that I have somehow outraged members of my species by considering them part of a species at all. And how often the special pleaders use my work as a distorted echo chamber for their own ideas!

"Observation" is the key word here. For a writer whose mind worked largely along the procedures of science and whose work often concerns itself with the act of seeing and with perspective, it seemed a peculiar trait of critics to make judgments so often without looking very carefully at what they were judging.

The political storm that was generated by the publication of *The Grapes of Wrath* was enormous, probably the greatest such controversy set off by a novel in modern times. It was enormous not only in the depth of feeling that it aroused but also in its duration—the controversy went on for a very long time as the novel reached the best-seller lists in 1939 and stayed on through much of 1940. At the heart of the debate were questions about its realism and the motivations of the author.

Just as Hyman, among others on the left, later felt compelled to call him "dishonest," so at the publication of *Grapes* did the conservatives in California, Oklahoma, and elsewhere throughout the country scream "Liar!" The press, dominantly conservative, pounded on the theme, publishing reports sponsored by such organizations as the Associated Farmers and testimonials from self-confessed Okies. Of course, the history of the period and such documents as the *La Follette Report* (produced by a U.S. Senate committee investigating farm-labor violence and working conditions) suggest that, if anything, Steinbeck's novel underplayed the suffering and brutality. But it got to the point in the spring of 1940, when at last Eleanor Roosevelt came to his defense, that he wrote to her, "I have been called a liar so constantly that sometimes I wonder whether I may not have dreamed the things I saw and heard."

For months the attacks continued in the press, and Steinbeck was besieged by hate mail. Nearly every chance encounter with neighbors in Los Gatos and old acquaintances from the Salinas area led him to believe, probably correctly, that he was surrounded by people who hated his guts. He was denounced in Congress as having a "twisted, distorted mind," threatened with bodily harm, constantly called directly or by implication a liar, a pervert, a Communist, and a traitor. The draft board in Monterey went out of its way to harass him; he was given the runaround by the U.S. Passport Office; he was turned down for a commission in the army as "politically unreliable." He was warned repeatedly by friends in law enforcement to keep a diary and never stay in a hotel alone. There were places he was warned not to go, and the threat to his life became so real that he sent (in an action that seems naïve today) information to the FBI to be used if he died or disappeared under mysterious circumstances.

Perhaps most painful of all were the rumors that were spread about him, painful because he could not prove their source, although he suspected the Associated Farmers, and could not fight back. It was said that he was a dope addict and a drunk, a sexual pervert (who filled his book with dirt so that it would sell), and, most depressing of all, that he was a Jew, a Zionist-Communist who had set out deliberately to destroy the United States. This rumor became so widespread that he got letters from all over the country that either repeated it as accusation or asked him about its truth.

It was particularly sad to him as an ultimate low in bigotry and hate, and when the Reverend L. M. Birkhead wrote on behalf of the Friends of Democracy to inquire about the rumor that *Grapes* was Jewish propaganda and that Steinbeck was a Jew, Steinbeck answered: "It happens that I am not Jewish and have no Jewish blood but it only happens that way. I find that I do not experience any pride that it is so." He would answer Birkhead's letter, because it was well meant, but no others: "Those who wish for one reason or another to believe me Jewish will go on believing it while men of good will and good intelligence won't care one way or another."

He had been called a Marxist so repeatedly that even the Marxists began to believe it, and he began to get appeals for money from Communist and Communist-associated organizations, as well as requests for permission to use his name for this or that "liberal" cause. Like the hate mail, this mail in all its insistence and presumptuousness was not only irritating but somewhat frightening—it was like being adopted without one's consent.

Following the composition of *Grapes*, he was exhausted. An infection spread throughout his body, crippling his back and one leg so badly that for nearly a year he had to have help getting in and out of a car or going up or down steps. Under the pressure, his marriage to Carol was falling apart, and all the time he was worried about retribution. His plan for his own salvation was to try to withdraw as entirely as possible from the political controversy that kept trying to draw him into its vortex and to turn, as he had before but on this occasion on a full-time basis, to the study of natural science. He read extensively in the history of science, spent hours every day he could looking through the microscope in Ed Ricketts's lab, went on collecting expeditions in the tide pools, and planned several extensive projects with Ed. Only one was fully realized before Ed's death, the collecting trip that resulted in *Sea of Cortez*.

Not long after his scientific study began to manifest itself in publication, the left, which had adopted him, decided to dump him. Steinbeck had shifted his focus from the working poor, and his ideas, which the left had missed or ignored, became for a time too obvious to overlook. Hyman, in reviewing *Sea of Cortez* for the *New Republic*, discovers that Steinbeck has been an ecologist all along, but he does not think it is a particularly important concept, nor does he find it remarkable that an American novelist is devoted to it. All this science business, this "rambling philosophizing," seems to him irrelevant and superficial, and he is annoyed with Steinbeck's social Darwinism, which condemns collectivism as eliminating "the swift, the clever, and the intelligent."

Next, caught up in the war effort, Steinbeck wrote *The Moon Is Down*, which aroused the ire of James Thurber for not being anti-Nazi enough. And for Hyman it marked a

confirmation of Steinbeck's turning from "social commitment." He had used in *Moon* the same scientific objectivity
as *In Dubious Battle*, but for Thurber and a few others,
with that subject matter there was no excuse for objectivity. Nazis should be depicted as monsters. Steinbeck's
treatment of the Invaders (the story is written as a generalized allegory of occupation) as ordinary men caught up in a
movement beyond their control and as "herd men" doomed
to destruction struck these critics as "soft." Indeed, Thurber
was certain that such softness might well help America lose
the war and that Steinbeck was aiding the Nazi cause—a
charge that Steinbeck, who had written the book out of pa-
triotism, found very hard to take.

Regardless of Steinbeck's feelings, the accusation might
have had some justification, harsh as it was in that climate,
except for Thurber's attitude: he is so certain and so terribly
self-righteous. A book review is not just a book announcement or public evaluation; it is also very often a public trial
of the author's worth, professional and sometimes personal,
and it is a letter from critic to writer. Thurber takes great
pleasure in holding up Steinbeck's book to public ridicule,
mocking it as only Thurber can mock, and then sending a
letter to the author saying, in effect. "You silly bastard." He
asks what people in Poland would think about such sentimental trash.

As it turned out, in respect to the war at any rate, Thurber
was wrong. The Poles never got to see the book, but the
Norwegians gave Steinbeck a medal for the contribution
the book had made to the morale of their resistance. The
book was circulated by typewritten manuscript and mim-
eographed copies throughout several countries in occupied
Western Europe, although possession of it was a crime
punishable by death. Everywhere he went after the war,
Steinbeck was entertained and toasted by members of the
underground. Having been proved wrong, did Thurber
apologize for his scathing condemnation not only of a book
but of a man? Of course not.

Steinbeck's alleged "softness" became a major issue with

The Moon Is Down, and with the publication of *Cannery Row* near the end of the war "sentimentality" became the new catchword of Steinbeck criticism. He *was* a sentimental man, as he himself freely admitted. He was genuinely moved by instances of kindness and sacrifice for others. When he was in Poland in 1963, he was asked by a reporter for *Polityka:*

> "What are the virtues you appreciate most in people?"
> "Gallantry," he answered.
> "Chivalry, courage?"
> "Yes, but this is not all, I also mean kindness, heartfelt kindness besides chivalry and courage; and all that is genuine, individual and unique in men."

For the political person on the right or left, such a value system puts too much emphasis on things of minor consequence. For him, to be "realistic" in writing means to apply a political perspective to life. To be "sentimental" means that the writer is not showing conditions to be bad enough so that the proper political conclusions become obvious.

When Steinbeck speaks so often of trying to see the "whole thing," he is not just speaking holistically of man's place in the pattern of nature; he is also speaking of completeness, being able to see all the parts. But being devoted to politics, just as being involved in religion or the search for "success," one puts on selective blinders. To be truthful about the world and about man, one must see that not only is there misery, hatred, and despair in the world, there is also joy, love, and gallantry. The hatred in *In Dubious Battle* is balanced by the love of *The Grapes of Wrath.* For some leftist critics viewing these novels in retrospect, *Battle* is realistic, while *Grapes* is contaminated by sentimentality.

Yet, while Jim Casy and Tom Joad were considered by many on the left to be radical heroes, the scientist protagonist of *Cannery Row,* a loner, evoked only their contempt. An idealized portrait of Steinbeck's friend Ed Ricketts, Doc personified many of the traits and attitudes that the author admired most—a calm acceptance of life in all its various manifestations, a kindness based on a realistic perception of human weakness, and a holistic philosophy tinged with a mystical veneration for all life. Joad, who comes to have social purpose, they could understand, but Doc, who seems to have no purpose, no political ideals, no belief in human progress, they could not.

Cannery Row is, its author announced at the outset, a fable, a scientific-flavored fairy tale, and as such it obviously irritated socially conscious critics who did not think Steinbeck was being sufficiently serious. The *New Republic* called Steinbeck "meretricious" and thought the book characterized by "technical archness, superficial characterization and boozy metaphysics." *Commonweal* decided that it all "smells of fish and reeks with kindness" and is "as sentimental as a book can be."

Because it certified the switch from the subject of farm labor, because it endorsed values inimical to those concerned with the "class struggle," and because it revealed more pointedly than ever before its author's major concerns, *Cannery Row* marked the turning point in the reception of Steinbeck's work. It has also become a kind of test case, separating those who have sought to use the novelist and make him conform to their own ideas and political convictions from those who, whether or not they have agreed, have had some genuine interest in what the author had to say. Almost without exception, critics specializing in the study of Steinbeck's work have found merit in the book, while generalist critics writing for major intellectual journals have scorned it.

Following *Cannery Row* there was a gradual amelioration of the hostility of the conservative press. Steinbeck, to escape the wrath of the political right and to give himself as much freedom as possible, deliberately chose "a big, reactionary paper," the *New York Herald Tribune,* in which to print his World War II dispatches. In 1947 he wrote a series for the *Herald Tribune* which provided a sympathetic view of war-torn Russia, which was later reprinted as *A Russian*

Journal. In the late 1950s and early 1960s, the *San Francisco Examiner*, also a Hearst publication, printed two of Steinbeck's memoir articles, and, signifying some kind of final salvation, in its obituary in December, 1968, the *National Review* forgave him for his attack on the free-enterprise system in *Grapes* and complimented him on his stand in favor of an unpopular war. Yet, through all this time, as a sort of inevitable ritual, *Time* regularly panned everything he wrote, and conservatives among Steinbeck's neighbors in the Salinas Valley, Monterey, and Los Gatos to this day curse his name. Also to this day, *The Grapes of Wrath* and *Of Mice and Men* remain among the books most commonly banned from schools and public libraries throughout the country.

But by far the most publicly expressed hostility for Steinbeck in later years has been that of the intellectual left. Although in the 1950s and 1960s it was no longer fashionable to make overtly political judgments about literature, the suspicion that there was still some political prejudice would seem justified on the basis of a wholesale, blanket rejection by leftist critics of everything the author wrote after *Sea of Cortez*. As the overtly political attack diminished, the ground was switched to the author's integrity, and he was frequently accused of writing potboilers to please the popular taste for pap, although, in fact, he never wrote fiction to make money. With such later novels as *The Pearl, East of Eden*, and *The Winter of Our Discontent* and the novelist's continuing emphasis on individual moral responsibility, "moralistic" became the new catchword. One suspects, however, that, for at least some of these critics, the real complaint behind the label was not that Steinbeck was dealing with morality but that he was not sufficiently condemning the evils of capitalism, was giving too much attention to the middle class, and was focusing too exclusively on the inward struggle of the individual. Furthermore, it irked such critics as Kazin, Hyman, and Mizener that to the very end of his career he saw the world essentially in biological, rather than in political-economic, terms.

Perhaps the true nature of the grudge the left held against him in his later years was most nakedly revealed at a press conference held in West Berlin in 1963, at the end of a long trip the author had taken behind the iron curtain. A questioner, whose stridency and ideological certainty strongly suggested that he was a Communist party "plant," tried to nail the author to the wall by asking directly why he had turned "from being a Marxist to a Puritan." The crowded auditorium was quiet as the novelist paused for a moment, then mildly replied, "I don't know what you mean. I've never been either." His novels of social reform, he said, "were stories of people, not political treatises."

There is good reason to believe that there was more than a little dishonesty in the criticism of Steinbeck and his work in this country during the last two decades of his life. Gratuitously violent attacks on such books as *Cannery Row*, *The Pearl*, *East of Eden*, and *The Winter of Our Discontent* pretended to be severe indictments of Steinbeck's aesthetic sins. But the nastiness of Hyman in the *New Leader* or of *Time* magazine would seem to have had little to do with whether these books were good or bad but rather with the novelist's values and politics, which both political poles found unpalatable. Not only was there dishonesty, but, considering the tradition that forbids an author to answer insult and slander, there was also a certain amount of cowardice.

The sad part of the pattern of violent political attack that followed the novelist was that it was a red herring. It detracted from the fact that he had a number of important things to say. As early as the mid-1930s he was talking about man living in harmony with nature, condemning a false sense of progress, advocating love and acceptance, condemning the nearly inevitable use of violence, and preaching ecology at a time when not even very many scientists cared about it. When he talked about the human "species" and the need to live in harmony with the whole of nature and the need to adapt (if homo sapiens does not, some other species will, he pointed out), he might as well have

John and Elaine at a reception held by a Swedish publisher following the
Nobel Prize ceremony, 1962. Courtesy of the John Steinbeck Library,
Salinas.

been talking Martian, as far as most literary critics were
concerned.

Throughout his career, John Steinbeck resisted tremen-
dous pressures to conform, pressures against independent
and unpopular thought, and against any expression of man's
condition which did not meet the political-philosophical
criteria of many of his professional readers. Some of the
things he wrote, particularly at the beginning and end of
his career, were failures or only partial successes. But he
never gave up his effort to write what he felt was true and
to write something different in approach and form with
every book. And he was never ever satisfied that what he
had written was good enough. He took an enormous amount
of abuse, much of it politically inspired, and he was the tar-

get of far more hostility than most artists could even imagine surviving. Yet he always went his own way. He never gave in, and he never sold out.

As the time for the publication of my book approached, I braced myself for my own reviews. I also became involved in a new publicity campaign. Some authors who write books that a publisher thinks may have a chance to become best sellers take what is called the "fourteen-city tour." Weary and wealthy, they appear on talk shows to complain about the wear and tear on their physical and mental well-being from such a demanding travel schedule. I had a two-city tour—San Diego, my home, and Los Angeles, a little over a hundred miles away, and I would have been glad to wear myself to a frazzle in more ambitious publicity efforts. I knew that it was not going to be repeated in the near future, if ever.

Most of my activity was not very glamorous, although there were a few highlights. I was invited to lunch with the editors and executives of the *Los Angeles Times* and went on a couple of Los Angeles TV and radio shows. My only "national exposure" was an interview by Bob Edwards on National Public Radio's "Morning Edition." I was a faithful listener to the program, particularly when I was in the mountains, where it was my only source of news and entertainment.

The interview was arranged to take place by satellite, Edwards in Washington, D.C., and I in the Los Angeles studios of NPR. I stayed overnight at a hotel and arrived at the studio about an hour and a half early. I was concerned to be on time, because the letter I had received had instructed me that there was a broadcast "window" for the transmission, starting a little after 8:00 A.M. and lasting only a half hour. I located the studio in a tall office building and then went to have breakfast. About 7:45, I returned to the studio, but no one was there. I sat on the floor and waited outside the door. At 8:14 a harried young woman, obviously late to work, dashed to the door, pulled it open, and disappeared. With hardly a word, she ushered me quickly into a soundproof room by myself with a huge mike on a boom in front of me. She gave me a large pair of earphones and said, "You'll hear Edwards' voice through here and just answer into the microphone," and then left.

A moment later I heard this voice, which I had heard innumerable times on my radio, talking. I was petrified. Always before I had had someone in front of me to talk to, but here I was alone, and it took me several moments to realize that the voice was actually talking to me and that I should say something. There was also a second or so delay as our voices went up to the heavens and came back down again thousands of miles away, and this was distracting. As I talked, I realized my voice was quavering—which had never happened before—and that completely unnerved me. Several times I began to answer questions, and before I had talked more than a few moments, I had forgotten what the question was. The interview was the worst I had ever given. I had done well on local stations, but I was clearly not ready for the big time.

About this time, I began to get reviews. Often they came in bunches from Viking, but I also got some from my agents, and occasionally a review was sent to me directly by the reviewer. I was looking forward to the *Monitor* review, certain in my mind by now that it would be *the* review that would do the book justice. When finally it came, I was shattered. There was almost nothing in it about the book itself, and I felt certain that my busy free-lance reviewer, Tom Wills, had simply not had time either to finish his reading or to do his homework with other publications about Steinbeck so that he would be able to evaluate what he was reading.

Instead of dealing with the book's writing and contents, and what I had discovered about Steinbeck, the review featured the opinion of Thom Steinbeck, of all people, that I had "manipulated people's personalities to put my father always in the right. I love my father very much, but he wasn't a deity." Wills had followed this lead, and the title of the review was, "Most Comprehensive Yet, but Marred by Bias." What really rankled was that the odds that Thom had actually read through the entire galleys, word for word, were in my view about a billion to one or more. Evidence for these odds came in Thom's "charge" in the review that I had not given enough space to Ed Ricketts, an accusation apparently designed to feed Ed's son's hostility. (In the book I had given Ricketts a mini-biography of a whole, very long chapter, plus substantial parts of other chapters—far more space than any other secondary character has ever received, so far as I am aware, in a modern biography.) The picture of Wills and what he had been doing, of his relations with Thom, Ed Ricketts, Jr., and Carol's husband, was becoming clearer and clearer as the review continued. It ended with a backhanded compliment that at least I had given Carol Steinbeck her due—she was so vital and talented, and had such an impact on Steinbeck's career, that she deserved a biography of her own. When Wills talked about Carol in the review, trumpets played "Pomp and Circumstance." Later, I found out that—guess who?—had become Carol's biographer.

My mother was deeply hurt by the review, my uncle, who worked for the *Monitor*, was completely silent on the matter, and Dick Allman was furious and wrote an angry letter to the newspaper, which, of course, was never published. At first I felt betrayed, but then when Wills called and with pleased voice asked me how I liked the piece, I realized that he was operating as a journalist writing what he thought was a "story" and that, as far as he was concerned, the story was contained not in the book but outside, in the reactions of a famous man's son. When I told him that it was by far the worst review that I had received, he was taken aback and said that he thought it was a very "balanced" report. He did quote me about how long I had worked on the book, but he did not quote from any of a hundred Steinbeck relatives or close friends who had known John far more intimately and longer than his son had—

Thom was six when John was almost fifty, near the end of his career, and writing *East of Eden*. Furthermore, after Thom was two, he lived almost exclusively with his mother and her family, all of whom were undyingly hostile to John. I was disappointed but had to admit to myself that, if I had been used, it was because I had allowed myself to be used. I also learned that, despite all the complaining the children of the famous may voice about trying to find their way in the shadow of their parent, what they say seems to have an instant credibility that on their own they don't seem to have to earn.

In the long run the *Monitor* review did not matter, and there was a happy ending after all. The biography evoked an enormous number of reviews, more than a hundred at last count, and the vast majority were positive. Reviews of the book were featured on the front pages of book sections in newspapers across the country—Los Angeles, San Francisco, New York, Boston, Chicago, and Dallas. I knew, however, that it wasn't my book or my writing that in themselves had prompted such an outpouring of attention and praise but that many literary people here and around the world felt that John Steinbeck was overdue. A good man and a fine writer had been beaten about the head and shoulders long enough.

Even though it wasn't primarily for me, I enjoyed the attention the book was getting. I was especially delighted when I got a copy of a front-page rave review in the *New York Times Book Review*, because I certainly didn't expect it. Few writers receive such a notice in their lifetimes, and I was ecstatic. I showed it to my wife, and we danced and sang about the house and celebrated by calling our relatives. But all the while I had the nagging feeling that my wife was celebrating something other than what I was celebrating.

Early in our marriage, when I first started the book, I used to chase my wife around the fireplace in the center of our house. She would yell and scream, and I would yell and scream, and our two little girls would stand by, cheering us on and laughing at us. Now, although our cheering section was grown and gone, I had the urge once again to chase Sue Ellen, and with an Indian war whoop I took out after her. Around and around we went, but only a few times before I caught her—too easily, I thought. Was she tricking me, or could she have slowed down that much in fifteen years?

Epilogue: The Spirit of a Writer

For years I had wandered through a forest of imperatives—to search for as much relevant information as possible, to organize a nearly endless array of details, to select those materials most pertinent to a truthful and well-balanced account, and to compose the most compelling narrative possible. Then, after making my way through the forest, I had to find my way through a swamp of controversy, trying to survive the shame of losing, at least in part, my artistic integrity and the gut-wrenching fear of losing my home and all my financial assets—as well as the guilt of leading my family to risk such a disaster. The journey did not allow much opportunity for meditation, not much time to consider the ultimate question that was the reason for the journey in the first place: Who, really, was this man?

What was the essence of him, or the spirit, that had led so many to become so devoted to his work? What was there about the quality of the man as reflected in his work that made him the most widely read by the people, by worker and intellectual, of the writers of his time? That enabled his work to endure vagaries of taste and fashion, constant denigration, banning, and censorship? Beyond the facts, the controversies, and the contradictions, the welter of a life in all its peculiarities, was there an essential message, a legacy?

If it was strange that, after all the effort I had made, I had not located and defined that essential spirit, it was even stranger that an answer came to me not in response to thinking about the man himself but several years later in the perspective of holding him up to the profile of another writer.

My initial thoughts about the matter came to me as little more than distractions during the writing of the biography:

while writing about John Steinbeck, I was constantly reminded of things I already knew about Ernest Hemingway.
They were so much the same in many ways that, as I dealt
with one thing and another in Steinbeck's life, echoes would
come shooting into my mind from my previous study of the
other author. How strange it was that such similar events
had taken place, I would think, or how odd that, coming
from such similar backgrounds, they should react so differ-
ently. And my mind would wander off into space, as I con-
templated the two writers. It was always more attractive to
dream, to contemplate, to mentally play with the possibilities than to force myself to tackle the writing problem
at hand.

Then, several years after I had finished the manuscript, I
was looking through some photographs of John's family, and
I was forcefully struck once again by the similarity of the
two writers' families and of the circumstances of their early
lives. It may have been the fashions of dress and grooming
or the style of photography, but as I looked at John's parents
in photos taken in the years just following their marriage, I
felt I had seen them before, so similar were they to the
Hemingways. The father in each family was tall, broad-
shouldered, and stern-looking, dressed in a long dark coat,
wing collar, and tie. I wondered, as I compared photographs, if the fathers had assumed an expression that they
thought appropriate to a formal occasion, or if they just
didn't—typical males—like having their pictures taken.

The large-bosomed, heavyset woman in the photos of
each family was dressed in a frilly, long-sleeved blouse, and
in some of the pictures, her hair was pinned up under a
broad-brimmed hat. The half smile on her round face contrasts with her husband's seriousness, and she seems to sit
there with all the patience in the world, with everything
under control.

It came to me that not only did Clarence and Grace
Hemingway and John Ernst and Olive Steinbeck look alike
in general features, but they held similar values: a Prot-
estant religiousness (the Hemingways were Congregation-

Clarence and Grace Hemingway, Ernest standing at his mother's left, ca. 1904. Courtesy of the John F. Kennedy Library, Boston, Massachusetts.

alists; the Steinbecks, Episcopalians); a sober, Victorian sense of propriety; and a typically upper-middle-class, turn-of-the-century devotion to respectability, the Puritan work ethic, and aesthetic culture. From such unlikely roots as these would come two writers whose images would shock our sensibilities and whose visions would shake our complacencies.

Although the reputations of Steinbeck and Hemingway rose and dipped throughout their careers, their popularity never wavered, either here or abroad, and so closely were their stars joined in the public mind that they were often confused with one another. Even the critics categorized them together, deciding that the slightly younger Steinbeck was a disciple of the older Hemingway—a suggestion that put Steinbeck's teeth on edge. And although they met only once, they appear to have been constantly aware of

John Ernst Steinbeck and Olive, ca. 1899. Courtesy of the Steinbeck Research Center, San Jose State University.

one another's presence on the literary stage, particularly during the mid-portion of their careers, from the late 1930s through the early 1950s.

The juncture, and occasionally blurred identities, of these two writers had its ironies. Although their backgrounds and the influences operating on them were remarkably similar, no two writers could have been more different in temperament. The similarities suggest something about the soil required in the American climate to produce the novelist who is judged to have spoken eloquently to his own time. The differences in background may provide some clues to why these writers took such widely divergent views of the world and man's place in it. Indeed, the major irony of their juncture is that each represented a philosophy of modern existence so fundamental, yet so opposite, as to be like the two sides of the same coin.

Both Hemingway and Steinbeck grew up in conservative small towns—Oak Park, Illinois, and Salinas, California— in the decades just before America's entrance into World War I. They were reared in similar two-story Victorian houses, grew up with three sisters (Hemingway also had a sister and a brother much younger), and had fathers devoted to nature and mothers devoted to the arts. As boys they had paper routes, took music lessons, and served in the church, Ernest as a choirboy and John as altar boy. Early in their lives both became adept at telling stories— Ernest, as Carlos Baker tells us, usually about himself as a swashbuckling hero, and John usually about ghosts, magicians, and leprechauns.

Both boys liked to dramatize their experiences and embroider on the truth, a tendency that stayed with them all their lives. As grown men, in their recollections they freely mixed fact and fiction, and neither could refrain from exaggeration or occasional fabrication in ordinary conversation. Their families became aware of their free play of fancy when the boys were quite young. Ernest's maternal grandfather warned his daughter that if her son "uses his imagination for good purposes, he'll be famous, but if he starts the wrong way, with all his energy, he'll end up in jail." On a similar occasion, after hearing a whopper from her son during a women's club meeting, Steinbeck's mother shook her head sadly and announced to her friends, "He'll either be a genius, or he'll amount to nothing."

The two youngsters discovered in storytelling a way of asserting themselves and impressing others. Hemingway seems to have been most concerned with showing adults he was brave and grown up (in his later fictions individual courage would, of course, become a major theme); Stein-

beck, with gaining recognition from his peers by demonstrating secret or special knowledge (in his writing the figures of the scientists, the magician, and the seer would
appear frequently). In their childhood stories they established a point of view that continued into their mature
work: Hemingway almost invariably wrote about himself,
either directly or indirectly, and Steinbeck wrote about the
emotions and problems of others.

The influence of family members helps explain the direction each boy would take later in life. Hemingway's male
relatives were storytellers, and his father loved to relate
the hunting exploits of his youth; he was not adverse to
boasting now and then about his genuine accomplishments
as a sharpshooter. On the other hand, it was Steinbeck's
mother who told him bedtime stories out of her Irish heritage, stories of enchanted forests, fairies, and magic. Of
these sources, the former was a public act, the latter a
shared secret, and the nature of these early experiences
may have been in part responsible for Hemingway becoming the most public of our major authors and Steinbeck one
of the most private.

Although the fathers of the two boys were subject to dark
depressions, and both felt at the end defeated by life, they
are, for the most part, a study in contrasts. Hemingway's
father could be truly stern, a man with a temper and a great
deal of pent-up violence. Although he knew his Christian
duty and performed acts of kindness and charity all his life,
he could also be dourly religious and intolerant. The senior
John Steinbeck looked forbidding, and he also had "keen,
piercing eyes that looked right through you when he was
serious" (in Madelaine Hemingway's words about *her* father), but in reality he was a gentle, quiet man whose kindness came less from religiousness than from his nature. As
one of John's sisters has said—a description that applied
just as well to her brother—"He suffered for other people's
problems."

Both Clarence Hemingway and John Ernst Steinbeck
were closely connected to nature, but their interests took

very different directions. The Steinbecks lived in town, but the father was a farmer at heart, usually keeping a cow (at his place of work as manager of the local flour mill), pigs, and horses, and he always had a large garden. Not only did he grow vegetables, but it was, as I have said, his pride to be able to have flowers all year long to place on the dining-room table. He taught all his children how to garden and brought them up to have love and respect for animals. He also taught them, out of his old-country German heritage, respect for the land and a sense of conservation—nothing should be wasted.

By contrast, although Clarence gardened and even ran a farm near his summer home, his real pride was in his fishing and hunting, particularly the latter, and in providing fresh game for the table. His German heritage had a different emphasis—concern for being a "real man" and demonstrating it in physical activity. He taught his boy to fish and hunt and camp out, and because of his troubled relations with his wife, the outdoors came to represent to his son, as it clearly represented to him, relief from womankind and freedom from domestic tyranny.

Flowers on the table and game on the table—the differences in role models appear to have contributed to the sons' differences not only in temperament and interests but in the subject matter and themes of their fiction as well.

From the time they were very young, Ernest and John accompanied their parents to summer homes on the water, where each learned to swim, hike, fish, and manage boats. The environments, however, were really quite different. Hemingway's experiences were on Walloon Lake, in upper Michigan, while Steinbeck's were at the seashore, in Pacific Grove, California. The woods are more often than the seashore thought of as masculine territory, and there is something much more manageable about a lake than an ocean, which may constantly remind the observer of his insignificance. Ernest was a boy, always active and usually with a gang, who could give and take a dare: Who can swim the farthest? Dive the deepest? John, often a loner, spent some

Ernest Hemingway at Walloon Lake, in upper Michigan, summer, 1912. Courtesy of the John F. Kennedy Library.

John on the "red pony," Jill, in the Salinas Rodeo Parade, 1913. From a *Salinas Index* photograph, courtesy of Mrs. John Steinbeck.

of his time wandering along the sand and through the rocks, stopping to watch and sometimes gather the little sea animals in the tide pools. Ernest, the doer and competitor, as soon as he was old enough struck out from his summer home into the nearby woods to hunt, fish, and camp. John, observer and collector, would much rather sit and watch the waves and daydream than do anything that required a lot of exertion.

The households of these two boys nurtured their artistic sensibilities in a variety of ways. There were plenty of books and magazines to sample, and early in their teenage years both turned to reading with a passion. Ernest's mother had been trained for the opera and gave voice lessons; John's mother had been a schoolteacher and played opera recordings on her Victrola while she was doing housework. Grace Hemingway also painted, while Olive Steinbeck was a great reader, of the classics as well as of current books, and did a bit of writing of her own. These families felt that artistic accomplishment was important and that people's lives could and should be enriched by the arts.

Beyond an affection for language and books, each boy picked up an affinity for another art form out of his home atmosphere which would influence his later development as a writer. Hemingway acquired an appreciation of painting, and his experiences with modern works in Paris in the mid-twenties would affect his style and form. His descriptions and scenes would be guided by a pictorial sense of spatial relationships; his style would become flat and understated, gaining texture from repetition and omission. On the other hand, Steinbeck grew in his appreciation of music. Just as his mother listened to opera while she was working around the house, he would play appropriate music while he wrote. Sound would become his primary stylistic consideration, and he would organize his books according to the patterns of musical composition.

While the mothers of these two writers provided the stimulus toward an interest in art, differences in their relations with their sons contributed to nearly opposite attitudes toward women, marriage, and family. Both mothers were domineering and socially conscious. But Grace Hemingway was not an active, hardworking woman; she often played the martyr, retiring to her room with a sick headache when things did not go her way, and she depended on servants or her husband to do the housework she thought beneath her. Olive Steinbeck was more cheerful and open, and she worked hard not only for her family but for various community and charitable causes.

Steinbeck's mother could be demanding, but she was also fun-loving. She and her son had many long discussions and arguments, during which they agreed to disagree about certain things, such as politics, whereas Ernest seems to have given up early in his teens trying to communicate with his mother except on a very formal basis. Although Olive, like Grace, had a strong sense of propriety, she was more tolerant (perhaps because she was better educated and better read), and she displayed far more loyalty to her son during the early years of his career, despite misgivings concerning his style of living and some of the subject matter of his fiction.

Grace Hemingway rejected her son's early work, joining with her husband to send back copies of the first book, *In Our Time*, that Ernest sent them, objecting to its low subject matter and vulgar expression. When *The Sun Also Rises* came out, she wrote to Ernest that she was glad to know the book was selling, although it seemed to her "a doubtful honor" to have written "one of the filthiest books of the year." She agreed with the judgment of her book study club that her son was "prostituting a great talent . . . for the lowest ends." On the other hand, when Olive's book club rejected her son's *The Pastures of Heaven* as "filth" (among other objectionable aspects, the book gave very generous treatment to two prostitutes, who provided, in the author's view, a valuable service to the community), she defended it and continued to carry it about town, displayed conspicuously under her arm. When she lay dying, some two years later, she pressed copies of her son's books on her nurses, recommending that they read them, for her son was "becoming a great writer."

Ernest and John went through small-town public education (John's high school graduating class was 24; Ernest's, 150). Both got decent grades, but neither distinguished himself as a scholar. Instead, responding to American high school values, they tried to distinguish themselves as athletes, but they were big, slow, and clumsy and did not perform very well. Both boys were known to their classmates for their humor and wisecracks, although neither was among the most popular boys in his graduating class.

Success and attention came to them as they excelled in writing. They each had two English teachers who found in them a special talent and encouraged it. On numerous occasions Hemingway and Steinbeck heard their English class writings read aloud to their classmates as models for emulation. And it may be that this encouragement and praise were key factors in persuading them to become writers. They appear to have come to this decision relatively early in their lives, about halfway through high school, and once made it was firm. It apparently never occurred to them from that point on to become anything else, although both sets of parents—despite their regard for literature—would have preferred that their sons continue on through college and become "professional men."

Ernest did a considerable amount of writing for both the high school newspaper, the *Trapeze*, and the literary magazine, the *Tabula*. His fiction, Carlos Baker notes, was for the most part "tough-minded, firmly plotted, original, and astonishingly free of those ineptitudes common to high-school writing." John did not have in his smaller school the same opportunities for publication, although he did write several pieces (in a prose that was also advanced for his age) for the one publication available to him, the yearbook, *El Gabilan*. Instead, after his sophomore year, he retired to his room on the second floor of his home to work on stories that he hoped to sell to national magazines. However, for some reason that he was later unable to recall, he sent them off under a pseudonym with no return address and then looked in the magazines, issue after issue, to see if they had been published.

This strange tactic would seem to reflect his later desire to keep his life and personality separate from his work in the belief that public knowledge of them would hinder his ability to write. Hemingway, who hustled to make a name for himself in school, went on, of course, to advertise himself shamelessly, perhaps in the belief that it would ensure his enduring success as a writer regardless of possible critical rejection.

As they grew into manhood, both Ernest and John rebelled against the Victorian respectability and restrictiveness of their early environments, but the targets of their rebellions were significantly different. Hemingway personalized his, pulling away from his parents, even coming to hate his mother, who represented for him all those forces that worked against his achievement of individuality and masculinity. Steinbeck generalized his, coming to hate Salinas and all that it stood for—narrowness, prejudice, and hypocrisy. All the rejections that he experienced as a child and a sensitive teenager he laid at the door of his community as a whole.

In their fiction both men became part of that broad movement of American writers during the first half of the century which sought to free the American spirit from the Puritan-Victorian repression which had imprisoned it. Hemingway concentrated on the condition of the individual, cut off from family, who finds it difficult to achieve a satisfactory and enduring love relationship. Steinbeck usually wrote about man in a family or man in a group that functions as a surrogate family. The individual is not alienated, but the family or group may be cast out or segregated from respectable middle-class society—and it is this society that he scorned. In its restrictiveness, narrow-mindedness, and greed, this society-at-large contrasts unfavorably to the relaxed, loving, and uncompetitive communities of Tortilla Flat or Cannery Row.

Out of their early experiences Hemingway and Steinbeck developed nearly opposite attitudes toward man's relationship with nature, and each, out of his own emotional needs, adopted a very different role as writer in our society. In his life and in his work, Hemingway expressed the Judeo-Christian perception of nature as subservient to human needs and the frontier attitude that nature is a challenge, an arena in which the male of the species proves his manhood. His ongoing efforts to dominate nature became the essence of his public personality. He became one of the best-known big-game hunters of his time, while, by contrast, Steinbeck—a nonviolent man—hated the very idea of killing animals for sport. Ernest was also declared by experts to be one of the two best deep-sea fishermen in the world. At the same time that Ernest was hauling in record marlin off Key West and Cuba, John was putting around the inlets and bays of Long Island in his motorboat trying, not always very successfully, to catch small fish for food.

In Hemingway's life, as in the metaphor of the bullfight in his work, the concept of the arena was important, for if one seeks to be the expert, the winner, the hero, he must have an audience to appreciate his expertise, acknowledge his triumphs, and admire his heroism. Hemingway's arena ranged from a changing circle of close friends (whom he seemed to keep only if they were properly admiring) to the world at large through the agency of *Time* and *Life* and other commercial magazines. He became the darling of *Time*, which praised nearly everything he wrote, including such clunkers as *To Have and Have Not*. The magazine loved him as the archetypal individual, a heroic personality it could effectively promote. His good looks, his adventures on safari, his brawls, and his friendships with movie stars made good copy, and his style of living fit the magazine's philosophy and politics.

Steinbeck, who lived privately and had few dramatic adventures, who wrote about man in his family attempting to live in harmony with nature, was antithetical in every way to the values of rugged individualism *Time* endorsed. It panned every one of his books, perhaps because it thought of him, inaccurately, as a Marxist (it used the code phrase "proletarian writer"). His emphasis on cooperation rather than competition was dull, just as his life seemed dull, and throughout his career, *Time* never gave him or his work a kind word until it wrote his obituary.

Hemingway's childhood need to be recognized and his teenage desire to be popular grew into an adult appetite for fame and publicity that seemed insatiable. He always had a quip for reporters and a smile for photographers; indeed, no other major writer before or since has been interviewed or photographed as often. The only writer ever to be elevated by the press to superstar status, Hemingway gave substance to the mid-twentieth-century mass-media version of the American dream—to grow up not to be president but to have your face on the cover of *Time* and *Life*.

Popularity was anathema to Steinbeck, who viewed writing as a private act, almost sacredly so, and who would have preferred to remain largely unknown and read by only a few. He was so shy that, except on a handful of occasions, he was unable to mumble more than a sentence to an audience. If Hemingway was the insider, always among the initiated, Steinbeck was the outsider who grew up out of loneliness and a sense of alienation to identify with the inarticulate, the handicapped, and the dispossessed. He regularly declined to be interviewed or photographed, and on those few occasions when he could not get out of an interview, he refused to talk about himself. On one occasion, just after he had achieved some fame in the late thirties and a publicity photograph had been circulated by his publisher against his wishes, he was recognized on the street in San Francisco, and the shock so nauseated him that he almost threw up on the spot.

Both writers were not only novelists but journalists throughout their lives, and one reason why Hemingway's exploits were so well known was that he publicized them himself. Seldom in Steinbeck's journalism do we see the writer and then only in a very self-effacing way. Both writers participated in World War II as correspondents, and both were involved in battle situations in which they displayed conspicuous courage, but Hemingway's actions in short order became known to the world, whereas Steinbeck's were known only to the men that he had been with. John was recommended for the Silver Star, but the navy declined to give the award to a civilian; Ernest was recommended for the Bronze Star, and through the pressure of his public stature and the help of officer friends, he actually received it.

Unlike Ernest, John felt very intimidated by his fellow journalists, usually doing everything possible to avoid talking to them, and above all, he didn't want to talk about himself. If an interview was scheduled, he was adept at inventing excuses, and if he was cornered (usually by some clever ruse of his publisher), he was adept at changing the subject. At the height of his fame when he was met at a European airport by a crowd of reporters, he would turn to his wife and beg her to go out and talk to them first, before he got off the plane, to "warm them up a little."

Steinbeck's talent was to efface himself both in life and in his work, to remain ordinary among ordinary people, working with them in the fields or listening to them around a campfire or in a diner. Hemingway's talent was to carry the burden of being extraordinary, and to carry it, despite disappointments and attacks of self-doubt, with courage and considerable style. Steinbeck sent out a message that, despite the pressures of modern life, of industrialism and materialism, it is still possible for human beings to understand and have compassion for one another. Hemingway sent out a message that, despite the pressures of modern life, its standardization and conformity, it is still possible for man to achieve the remarkable, to maintain his individuality and be true to himself.

The difference in focus of their fictions can be defined, in part, by statements each author made concerning the origins of the modern American novel. Hemingway declared it all started with Mark Twain's *The Adventures of Huckleberry Finn*, while Steinbeck felt it came out of the fiction of Sherwood Anderson. In Twain's novel, Huck preserves his individuality and masculinity from the civilizing schemes of Aunt Sally by escaping to the frontier. In Anderson's *Dark Laughter*, a natural and relaxed way of life as signified by the dark laughter of the Negro is contrasted to the unnatural and repressive strictures of middle-class society; and in his *Poor White*, a man and his wife reject the lure of the new industrialism to stay with a richer life close to the land.

In Hemingway's fiction, man's stance toward nature is somewhat more complex than that expressed in the author's life, but the emphasis is still on the ultimate domination of the external world by acts of hunting and killing. The Hemingway character may feel at home in nature and be fond of its benign features, as is Nick Adams in "Big Two-hearted River," written at the beginning of the writer's career, and Santiago in *The Old Man and the Sea*, near the end. He may even feel so close to it at times that he identifies with it, as Nick and the old man mentally take the part of the fish in each story. Both men, however, catch their fish and, in doing so, prove something about their skill and endurance. And neither is so close to nature that he does not think of it as an adversary, dangerous and even treacherous. The Hemingway protagonist feels close to nature not because he feels a part of it but because, like the bullfighter, he has studied it and is an expert in dealing with it.

By contrast to Hemingway himself, a man of charisma generally surrounded by cronies and beseiged by visitors, and a man with an enormous sense of competition who nearly always won whatever contest he entered, his protagonists seem to reflect his deepest fears about living in a dark, threatening world. Even in the company of friends or with lovers, his central characters are lonely men and, ultimately, losers. They are existential hero-victims cut off from intimacy of any lasting sort with either man or nature. They take whatever comfort or pleasure they can in the moment, in playing out as well as possible the game of life and

love, or, minimally, in securing a defensive position in which
they can survive emotionally. The condition is most dramatically illustrated by the older waiter in "A Clean, Well-
lighted Place": man is surrounded by darkness, "nada," and
the best he can hope for is to be able to survive with some
dignity. It is, of course, death, extinction of the self, that
these characters fear, and it may be that the same fear in
Hemingway drove him to such an unrelenting search for
literary immortality.

Steinbeck was also concerned with survival, but in a biological sense, rather than egocentrically. Unlike Hemingway, he was not a very competitive man, and his relations
with nature were based on a desire to understand and cooperate with the environment rather than dominate it.
If Hemingway played the part of Deerslayer, the white
hunter, then Steinbeck played Chingachgook, the native
American who felt a kinship with all of nature. In all its suffering, the Hemingway protagonist tells us, humanity is
important; in Steinbeck's work humanity is but a speck in a
very large universe—if man suffers, it is precisely because
he thinks he is more important than he is. By refusing to
see himself as primarily a biological entity, related to other
animals and the ecological whole, man not only suffers but
makes everything around him suffer also.

Where Hemingway was a talker, Steinbeck was a listener; where Hemingway was drawn toward the action to
participate, Steinbeck was drawn toward it to observe.
During his middle years, Steinbeck devoted much of his
time to study of the life sciences and observation of the eco-
system of the littoral, but that was only part of a life spent
essentially as a scientist and scholar. He had an unquench-
able curiosity about nearly everything and never lost a little-
boy wonder at what he discovered. He was delighted one
day, while reading medieval manuscripts at the Pierpont
Morgan Library, to find a crab louse embedded in the
ink—he had been examining the calligraphy with a magnifying glass. If Hemingway was always the maestro, the
tutor, who constantly required—as his younger brother has

said—a spiritual kid brother around to instruct and impress, then Steinbeck was always the learner, a man consumed by a desire to see things clearly, to see them in the context of the whole and to understand.

Out of his personality Hemingway projected a character who is solitary, suffering, and heroic; out of his, Steinbeck projected a character who is admirable not for what he does or what he undergoes but for what he is—the qualities of love and acceptance he expresses. Steinbeck's self-characters (as he called them), contrary to Hemingway's, are always looking outward, always concerned for others. They also differ in that they do not always have center stage but are sometimes minor characters who, like Doc Burton of *In Dubious Battle*, function primarily as observers. In the novel Burton explains to the Communist organizer, Mac, that, even though he is willing to give medical treatment to the strikers, he doesn't want to take sides in the dispute because he wants to be able to stand back in order to see the whole picture. Jim Casy, in *The Grapes of Wrath*, wants to join the Joads on their trek to California because he senses that something big is happening in the country, and he wants to observe and understand it.

A crucial difference in experience between the two writers came as a result of a two-and-a-half-year difference in their ages. Hemingway went to war and was seriously wounded, and, as Philip Young has suggested, the author and his fictional counterparts seem to have carried that wound and its resulting anxiety with them so that their lives were etched with recurring uncertainty and dread. Steinbeck, too young for the war, spent much of his youth working on farms and in the forest. His sympathetic descriptions of farm life and farm communities in works like *The Long Valley* and *Of Mice and Men* are among the best in American literature.

Steinbeck and his self-characters appear to have been so closely tied to the earth and its rhythms that for them death became but another part of nature's ongoing processes (he quoted Ecclesiastes to his doctor before he died). Hemingway, the hunter, soldier, and expatriate; Steinbeck, the farmer, student of nature, and local colorist of the American scene—nothing could be more in contrast than the characters that each has projected from himself, the one advocating courage and expertise in order to survive as an individual, the other advocating clear perception and loving acceptance in order that we might survive as a species.

The two writers did not know each other personally, although they had a number of friends, such as the photographer Robert Capa, in common. Both writers were nearly silent about each other's work in public; however, as one might expect from their personalities, Steinbeck spoke very well in private of Hemingway's work, referring to him several times in letters as "in many way . . . the finest writer of our time," whereas all of Hemingway's references in his letters are disparaging of Steinbeck as a popular and prolific writer. Perhaps this reaction came in response to the precipitous rise in Steinbeck's stock during the period from the publication of *In Dubious Battle* in 1936 to that of *The Grapes of Wrath* in 1939, at a time when Hemingway was writing little and was accused by many critics of not being sufficiently concerned with serious social issues. Until the late forties, when Faulkner's reputation began its climb, there is no doubt that Hemingway considered Steinbeck his main rival for what he called the "championship."

The only correspondence between them was one letter from Steinbeck, who in 1939 wrote of his admiration for Hemingway's technique in the story "The Butterfly and the Tank." This expression of admiration appears to have led indirectly to the famous meeting in 1944 between the two at Tim Costello's restaurant in New York, arranged by mutual friends at Hemingway's request. Considering the younger writer's shyness, it is not surprising that only a few words were exchanged—Hemingway took center stage, and Steinbeck hung back as one of several observers.

Included in the party was John O'Hara, who had with him an antique walking stick Steinbeck had given to him.

As they were standing at the bar, Hemingway contended scornfully that O'Hara's stick was not really a blackthorn. When O'Hara protested that it was, the other novelist bet him fifty dollars he could break it and proceeded to pull it down over the top of his head, splitting it in two. O'Hara was mortified, and Steinbeck, standing in the background, thought the whole incident stupid. For several years thereafter, Steinbeck held very ambivalent feelings about an author whose work he admired but whose behavior he detested. Later, when the rivalry between Hemingway and Faulkner became intense, the Californian commented in disgust that the two seemed to be "fighting over billing on a tombstone."

For his part, Hemingway continued to be unimpressed by the work of the younger novelist. The only recorded comment of a specific nature came to John in 1948, when his editor, Pascal Covici, passed on a remark heard by a third person: "Hemingway said he could not read Steinbeck any more after the last scene in *Grapes of Wrath* wherein the starving man seeks food at the breasts of the dying woman. Hemingway said that 'aside from anything else, that's hardly the solution to our economic problem.'" Steinbeck wrote back to Covici, "Mr. Hemingway's analysis is not quite valid, but very funny." The older writer may have been exercising his wit, but he also seems to have missed the point, since in his biological metaphor Steinbeck had presented what he thought *was* the solution to an economic system based on selfish possessiveness.

Again, as one might expect, Steinbeck had a somewhat better understanding of what Hemingway was saying in his fiction than the other way around, although his admiration was not uncritical. Hemingway's witticism at the expense of *The Grapes of Wrath* seems not to have embittered its author when, three years later, he wrote in the manuscript of *East of Eden:*

In my time Ernest Hemingway wrote a certain kind of story better and more effectively than it had ever been done before.

He was properly accepted and acclaimed. He was imitated al-most slavishly by every young writer, including me, not only in America but in the world. He wrote a special kind of story out of a special kind of mind and about special moods and situations. When his method was accepted, no other method was admired. The method or style not only conditioned the stories but the thinking of his generation. Superb as his work is, there are many things which cannot be said using it. The result of his acceptance was the writers did not write about those things which could not be said in the Hemingway manner, and gradually they did not think them either.

This passage is part of a long digression (excised before the manuscript was published) which is an apologia for writing a novel that may not fit its readers' expectations. He was writing *East of Eden* in a manner more like that of Fielding than modern taste, conditioned by the tough, el-liptical style of Hemingway, might allow. In his anticipation of criticism that the book was too slow, digressive, and talka-tive, Steinbeck was right. Whether or not the criticism was prompted by Hemingway's conditioning is a moot question, but certainly Steinbeck felt that it was, and he shared with a number of other novelists a resentment of the narrowing of taste caused, in their view, by Hemingway's influence.

That he himself had been influenced in his writing by the older writer is an admission he had never before made, publicly or privately. Up through World War II he had al-ways claimed, when asked about such an influence, that the only thing by Hemingway he had read was "The Killers" and that he had refused to read any more. He was so stunned by the mastery of the story, he would recall, that he decided not to read the author's work again for fear he would be in-fluenced inadvertently. Yet this was not true, as the let-ter about "The Butterfly and the Tank" and comments to friends in unguarded moments about other Hemingway works indicate.

He was trying to protect himself from being considered a disciple of Hemingway, just as Hemingway much earlier had hotly denied the palpable influence of Sherwood Anderson (an influence that he never could bring himself to acknowledge). But Hemingway's personality was so dominating and his style so commanding that they pulled Steinbeck into his orbit regardless of Steinbeck's conscious resistance. Despite his dislike of the Hemingway public persona, he found himself drawn to identify with it to some extent, just as so many others at the time found themselves entranced, whether they wanted to be or not.

When Hemingway was mistakenly reported killed in January, 1954, in a small plane crash in Uganda, the news came to John and his wife while they were vacationing in the Caribbean. Deeply moved, John went out to walk by himself along the beach for several hours, and by the time he got back, his wife was able to rush out to greet him with the corrected bulletin that Hemingway had survived. Rather than relieved, John was almost angry as he said, "Wouldn't you know! . . . Isn't that just like him, to scare us that way?"

In the mid-1940s, both men at nearly the same time began to wear beards, and Steinbeck, defensive at the coincidence, made a point of telling everyone that he had grown his because he had skin problems. Later in their lives, however, when both once again had beards, Steinbeck was occasionally asked, "Mr. Hemingway, may I have your autograph?" and in good humor he would sign "Ernest Hemingway." Fortunately for us, however, these were two very different men. They embodied in their almost parallel careers two contrasting ways of looking at the modern world, presenting to us a choice of dangers and a choice of courses of action.

Steinbeck suggested to us that we can either husband our resources, maintain an intimate relationship with the earth and its creatures, and learn to care for each other in time of need or perish in our blind egotisms, our selfish competitiveness, or our self-hatreds. Steinbeck, the farmer. Hemingway suggested that we must learn to master our environment, compete successfully in the arenas of society and nature, and have the courage to face alone the certain hardships that living entails, or we can be victimized by our surroundings, be forced to surrender our freedom and lose our individual identities, and be enslaved by our fears and illusions. Hemingway, the hunter.

Farmer and hunter—two opposing, traditional roles that date back to prehistory and still compete for our allegiance in the modern age. Steinbeck and Hemingway—between them they would seem to have embodied the fundamental values of the American character. If this is so, we may be able to discern in their fictions the moral alternatives before us, not only as individuals but as a society.

Index

DATE DUE